DATE DUE

LASERS

NEW EDITION

SCIENCE & TECHNOLOGY IN FOCUS

LASERS

N E W E D I T I O N

The Technology and
Uses of Crafted Light

Charlene W. Billings
and
John Tabak, Ph.D.

Facts On File
An imprint of Infobase Publishing

LASERS: The Technology and Uses of Crafted Light, New Edition

Facts On File, Inc.
An imprint of Infobase Publishing
132 West 31st Street
New York NY 10001

Library of Congress Cataloging-in-Publication Data

Billings, Charlene W.
Lasers: the technology and uses of crafted light / Charlene W. Billings and John Tabak.—New ed.
p. cm. — (Science & technology in focus)
Includes index.
New [rev.] ed. of: Lasers: the new technology of light. c1992.
Summary: Explains what lasers are and how they work and examines their various uses.
ISBN 0-8160-4784-7
1. Lasers—Juvenile literature. 2. Lasers. I. Tabak, John. II. Title. III. Series.
TA1682.B55 2006
621.36'6—dc22   2005033798

Facts On File books are available at special discounts when purchased in bulk quantities for businesses, associations, institutions, or sales promotions. Please call our Special Sales Department in New York at (212) 967-8800 or (800) 322-8755.

You can find Facts On File on the World Wide Web at http://www.factsonfile.com

Text design by Erika K. Arroyo
Cover design by Nora Wertz
Illustrations by Richard Garratt

Printed in the United States of America

MP MSRF 10 9 8 7 6 5 4 3 2 1

This book is printed on acid-free paper.

To James Douglas, who has never given me a piece of bad advice. Yet.

CONTENTS

ACKNOWLEDGMENTS

John Tabak is deeply appreciative to Frank Darmstadt, executive editor, for his many helpful suggestions and encouragement.

Special thanks to Penelope Pillsbury and the staff at the Brownell Library, Essex Junction, Vermont, for their willingness and skill in helping to research several important topics during the preparation of this book.

INTRODUCTION

Lasers are extraordinary devices, and they have an extraordinary history. Gordon Gould invented the laser about 50 years ago, but the science upon which the invention was founded was published about 100 years ago. In theory, lasers could have been invented anytime in the interim, but most scientists exhibited no interest in the topic because they thought that such a device was impossible to create. When the laser was finally invented, others attempted to claim priority, leading to one of the longest, most convoluted lawsuits in the history of the U.S. Patent Office. Today, all questions of priority have finally been settled.

When the first lasers were created, they represented a new type of engineering, one that, for the first time, mixed more traditional electrical engineering with concepts from the branch of physics called quantum mechanics. Since the 1930s, scientists had known the broad outlines of the theory of quantum mechanics, a theory that offered new insights into the nature of matter and light. Harnessing these ideas to produce useful consumer devices had, however, proved difficult. The laser was the first consumer device to make use of insights from this highly theoretical branch of science.

Today, lasers are everywhere. Most of us have several in our homes. They can be found in computers, where they are used to read and burn CDs and DVDs. In fact, all CD and DVD players use lasers, and many of us have laser printers as well. Lasers can be found at the checkout counter of most stores, where, together with computers, they make modern inventory control possible. They are in hospitals, where they are used in place of scalpels, and in certain factories, where they are used in place of drills, saws, scissors, and more traditional welding apparatus. Lasers play an important role in communications technology, where light waves increasingly supplant radio waves as carriers of information, and they play a vital role in science, where laser-based measuring devices have enabled scientists to collect millions of highly accurate measurements at relatively low cost. Frequently, lasers are used to perform tasks that cannot be accomplished in any other way. It is difficult to overestimate how dependent society has become on these devices.

Despite their ubiquity, most people are unfamiliar with the basic science of lasers, which depends on some not very well known properties of light, and some elegantly simple design concepts. Even after one appreciates how a laser beam is created, however, there is still the matter of the light itself. Consider these questions:

- What makes laser light special? (It is not the color. Although most of the lasers that we see emit red light, different lasers emit light in different colors, and some of the most common lasers emit beams that are invisible.)
- Why can laser light drill, cut, and weld, but ordinary light cannot?
- If lasers are so effective, why are they not even more widely used? What are their limitations?
- How are lasers employed to solve various technological and scientific problems?

These are some of the main questions addressed in this book.

It is important to bear in mind that some of the properties of lasers, even "ordinary" lasers, lie far outside our ordinary experiences. The units of measurement with which most readers of this book are accustomed—measurements expressed in terms of feet and inches and minutes and hours—are poorly suited to a description of lasers. Lasers have been created that shine for quadrillionths of a second and drill holes a small fraction of a millionth of an inch across. Common units of measurement were not created for such phenomena, and they are too awkward to use as their description. It is, therefore, necessary to employ the metric system together with a series of prefixes chosen to facilitate the description of the extremely small and the extremely brief. These prefixes are defined in the text and summarized in an appendix at the back of the book for ease of reference. With a little patience the reader will quickly master the system.

Finally, the field of lasers is still a work in progress. Despite their many applications, engineers and scientists continue to discover new, and often important, uses for lasers. They also continue to produce even more exotic lasers: X-ray lasers, lasers that shine for very brief instants of time, and lasers powerful enough to create temperatures and pressures that rival those of the interior of the Sun are only a few examples of evolving laser technology. But as important as lasers are now, there is little doubt that they will be even more important in the future.

1

THE NATURE OF LIGHT

Laser light is first and foremost a type of light. It has much in common with other types of light. The same concepts and vocabulary that scientists use to describe fluorescent light, sunlight, and firelight, for example, are also used in the study and description of laser light. To be sure, laser light is in certain ways very special. It can, for example, be used to drill neat holes in diamonds. But because it has so much in common with other types of light, it is necessary to understand some very general properties of light in order to understand what laser light is and what distinguishes laser light from other types of light.

At its most basic level, light exhibits two extremely important properties. First, light is energy in motion, and it moves with astonishing speed. Galileo Galilei (1564–1642), the 17th-century Italian physicist and one of the founders of modern science, attempted to measure the speed of light with this simple experiment: One night, he placed one observer on one hill and a second observer on a second hill several miles away. Both observers were equipped with lanterns. They covered their lanterns. When they were both ready, the first observer uncovered the first lantern. The light radiated out from the top of the first hill. When it reached the top of the second hill, the second observer detected it and uncovered the second lantern. The light from the

Thomas Edison's 1879 lamp. The first laser, created 81 years after the first lightbulb, brought about a revolution in the way that light is used. [SSPL/ The Image Works]

second lantern radiated outward, and some of that light was then detected by the first observer back on the first hill. The first observer noted the time elapsed from when the first lantern was uncovered to the time the light of the second lantern was detected back at the first hill. Galileo hoped that in this way he could measure the time it took the light to make the round-trip journey from hill one to hill two. (Dividing the round-trip distance between the lanterns by the elapsed time as measured by the first observer equals the speed of light—at least in theory.)

Unfortunately for Galileo, the light traversed the distance between the hills so much faster than the observers could react that virtually the entire time that elapsed between when the first observer uncovered the first lantern to when the first observer detected the light from the second lantern was due to the reaction time of both observers. Galileo was, therefore, unable to reach any conclusion about the speed of light. In fact, the second observer would have had to stand on the Moon for this method to have a chance of detecting the speed of light, but the theory behind the experiment is sound. Today, Galileo's experimental setup is frequently used—not to measure the speed of light, which is now well established—but *given the speed of light*, to measure the distance between hills and other objects.

In a vacuum, light travels 186,000 miles per second (300,000 km/s). (If Galileo had been able to place the second observer on the Moon, the first observer would have detected a delay of approximately two and one half seconds from the time the first lantern was uncovered to the time that the light of the second lantern became visible to the first observer.) But light is not just fast. The speed of light in a vacuum is a sort of universal speed limit. Nothing can be accelerated past the speed of light. Keep in mind, however, that remarks about the speed of light apply only to the speed of light in a vacuum. Light travels a little slower through air than through a vacuum, and little slower still through glass than air, for example. Nevertheless, phenomena involving light, and lasers in particular, happen quickly, because they happen at light speed.

To repeat: *Light is energy in motion.* When light ceases to move, it ceases to be light. When a car is left out in the Sun with its windows up, the interior becomes quite hot. Energy enters the car in the form of sunlight. (That is, of course, how it is able to pass through the windows—windows are transparent to light.) When the light strikes the upholstery, some of it is reflected, but most of it is absorbed and so ceases to be light. The energy that entered the car in the form of light is now re-radiated into the interior of the car in the form of heat. Because the windows are not transparent to heat, the temperature in the car begins to increase. As engineers have developed increasingly fine control over lasers, they have learned to transfer energy from one place to another in a concentrated beam at 186,000 miles per second (300,000 km/s).

The second important and very basic property of light is that it conveys information, that is, when light from an object enters our eye or some device—a camera, for example—that ray of light tells us something about where it has been. The information is always at least a little outdated, however, because it takes some time for the light to travel from one place to another. The delay is so slight that it is usually described as negligible—meaning that other sources of measurement error are usually much larger than the error made in failing to account for the finite speed of light. But in astronomy, where the distances involved are often huge, the time it takes for light to travel from one point to another (and so convey information from one point to another) is significant. Consequently, astronomers never observe how things *are*—information, too, does not travel faster than light—rather, they are forever observing how things *were* when the light that constitutes the image of the object under observation first began its journey to Earth.

It was, in fact, an astronomer who first successfully estimated the speed of light by making use of the great distances between planets. In 1675 the Danish astronomer Ole Roemer (1644–1710) carefully timed the motions of the moons of Jupiter when Jupiter and Earth were relatively near each other in space. Using these data, Roemer predicted when a Jovian eclipse would occur six months later when Jupiter and Earth were relatively far apart. At the predicted time, Roemer turned his telescope skyward and observed the eclipse occurring approximately 16 minutes later than he predicted. The reason? The image of the eclipse— that is, the information about the eclipse—took 16 additional minutes to traverse the greater distance from Jupiter to Earth that resulted from Earth's motion about the Sun. Information, like energy, is "light bound"; it can travel as fast as light but no faster.

At this point things become more complicated because careful observation reveals that light is a very complex and exotic phenomenon. Scientists discovered this early in the history of modern science. The Dutch physicist and mathematician Christiaan Huygens (1629–95) noticed certain properties of light and asserted that light is composed of waves. The English physicist and mathematician Sir Isaac Newton (1643–1727) noticed other properties of light and asserted that light is composed of particles. At the time these assertions seemed to be mutually exclusive—that is, scientists believed that the description of light as a wave and the description of light as a stream of particles could not both be correct. They believed that at most only one of the descriptions would stand up to experimental tests. Nevertheless, over time, evidence accumulated for both ideas.

It was not until the 20th century that scientists resolved the problem of the nature of light by learning to perceive it as having a *dual* nature; that is, there are circumstances in which light behaves as a wave and other circumstances in which it behaves as particles. Making this statement precise is one of the great triumphs of 20th-century physics. Light is a much more complicated phenomenon that it first appeared.

In order to understand lasers it is necessary to understand a little about both aspects of light—light as a wave and light as a particle.

The Wave Nature of Light

Because a light wave cannot be directly observed, it helps to think about water waves. Imagine a large circular tank of calm water. In the center of the tank is a vertical stick that extends partway into the water. If the stick is repeatedly raised and lowered into the water in a regular way, it will give rise to a series of regularly spaced waves that radiate outward from the stick. A small observer standing on a small platform situated in the water and located some distance from the stick would see wave crest after wave crest pass by. The view would resemble the

Christiaan Huygens (1629–95), Dutch mathematician and physicist, was the first to propose the wave theory of light. [Library of Congress, Prints and Photographs Division]

illustrations on the top of page 6. To describe this regular wave, one might talk about the height of each wave. The height of a wave is called its *amplitude*, and the amplitude is one-half the distance from peak to trough—one-half because the height of the undisturbed water is halfway between a wave trough and a wave crest.

Another important characteristic of the passing water waves is the distance between each wave crest—and notice that because the wave is so regular the distance from crest to crest is exactly equal to the distance from trough to trough—and this distance is called the *wavelength*

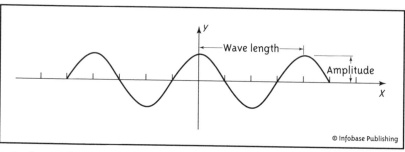

A simple waveform. Notice that the distance from trough to trough is the same as the distance from peak to peak, and that the amplitude indicated in the drawing is half the distance from peak to trough.

of the wave. The wavelength is often represented with the Greek letter λ, pronounced "lambda." Closely related to the wavelength is the concept of *frequency*, which is the number of times a wave crest passes the observer per unit time. The relationship between frequency and wavelength is an easy one: The frequency multiplied by the wavelength equals the speed of the wave. In the case of light, the frequency times the wavelength equals the speed of light in a vacuum. (Unless stated otherwise, whenever the speed of light is mentioned in this book, it will always mean the speed of light in a vacuum.)

The relationship between frequencies and wavelengths is simple enough to sum up in a single algebraic equation, and because articles and books about lasers, including this one, often use both the terms *frequency* and *wavelength* in describing light, it is better to see the equation now:

$$c = \lambda \nu$$

where the letter c represents the speed of light, the Greek letter λ represents the wavelength, and the Greek letter ν, pronounced "new," represents the frequency. Notice that given the frequency ν, the wavelength λ, can be obtained by dividing c, the speed of light, by ν. Alternatively, given the wavelength λ, the frequency ν can be obtained by dividing c by λ.

To return to the discussion of the water waves: Changing the frequency with which the stick in the imaginary tank is moved up and down changes the frequency of the resulting waves. But light waves also have frequencies. The eye perceives light waves of different frequencies as different colors. Higher frequency light waves, that is, light waves of shorter wavelengths, appear to humans' eyes as blues and violets. Lower frequency light waves are perceived as reds and oranges.

William Herschel (1738–1822), German-born English astronomer, detected invisible electromagnetic rays by passing sunlight through a prism. In addition to the usual rainbow of colors, he found that if he positioned a thermometer just beyond the red portion of the spectrum, the thermometer showed an increase in temperature. He had discovered infrared waves. [Ann Ronan Picture Library/HIP/The Image Works]

Light waves are part of a much larger collection of *electromagnetic waves*, waves of electrical and magnetic energy that traverse a vacuum at the speed of light. The set of electromagnetic waves also includes radio waves, infrared rays, ultraviolet rays, X-rays, and gamma rays. Light waves are special because they are the only electromagnetic waves that are visible to the human eye. Infrared rays, for example,

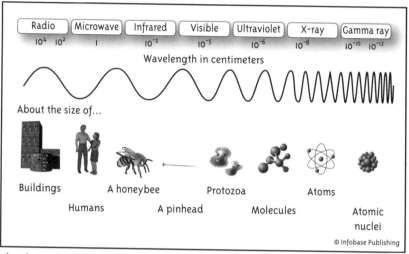

Radio	Microwave	Infrared	Visible	Ultraviolet	X-ray	Gamma ray

$10^4 \quad 10^2 \qquad 1 \qquad\qquad 10^{-2} \qquad 10^{-5} \qquad 10^{-6} \qquad 10^{-8} \qquad 10^{-10} \quad 10^{-12}$

Wavelength in centimeters

About the size of...

Buildings   A honeybee   Protozoa   Atoms

    Humans   A pinhead   Molecules   Atomic
                                                           nuclei

© Infobase Publishing

The electromagnetic spectrum. There is enormous variation in the lengths of electromagnetic waves.

have wavelengths that are a little longer than the wavelength of red light and so are invisible to the unaided eye, but infrared lasers are quite common. Ultraviolet rays, by contrast, have wavelengths that are a little shorter than the wavelengths of purple light, so they, too, are invisible, but they are important nonetheless. Ultraviolet rays, for example, are the electromagnetic rays responsible for sunburn. The same concepts of wavelength and frequency that are used to describe the properties of light waves are also used to describe the properties of all other electromagnetic waves. See the diagram above for more information on electromagnetic waves.

Light waves are seldom as simple in structure as the waves in the tank of water described previously. In fact, if it were possible to observe the waveform that everyone recognizes as sunlight or the light waves emanating from an incandescent bulb, for example, one would not see a regular waveform of the type described in the preceding paragraphs of this section. The reason is that most light, including sunlight, is composed of many different wavelengths of light—that is, many different waveforms—mixed together. This can be observed directly: Passing sunlight through a prism causes the sunlight to separate into its component wavelengths. A quick examination of the resulting *spectrum* of colors will show that every color of the rainbow is present in sunlight, and because the human brain perceives different wavelengths as different colors, this demonstrates that sunlight is composed of not one wavelength of light but many different wavelengths.

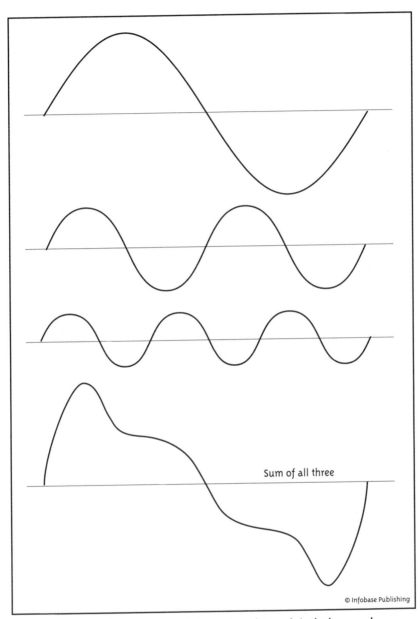

When the three simple waves are added together, the result is the less regular waveform on the bottom.

Passing sunlight through a prism and producing a rainbow also demonstrates that light waves of different wavelengths are capable of occupying the same space at the same time. Rather than one wavelength excluding all others, all wavelengths add together to produce light that is the combination of all the component waves. If blue light is combined with yellow light of a certain intensity, or amplitude, the resulting combination appears green. If many colors are combined, the result is white light. To do this graphically with two waves, for example, simply draw the two (simple) waves over the same interval. (As with the water waves described earlier, "zero height" is the height midway between the crest and the trough.) Finally, combine the heights of the two waves at each point. If a trough of one wave coincides with the peak of a second wave, the height of the resultant wave at that point will be less than the height of the peak of the second wave but higher than the trough of the first wave. The same principles apply to any number of waves. See the illustration on page 9 to see how this is done. Combining light waves of different wavelengths and different amplitudes can result in some very complicated waveforms, but the principles involved are exactly those used to combine two simple waveforms. That electromagnetic waves can combine, or mix, in this way is an important and characteristic property. It is called *interference.*

To make the concept more concrete, one can hear sound waves interfere with one another by listening to musicians tune their instruments. When two instruments—or two strings on the same instrument—are slightly out of tune relative to each other, the wavelengths of the sound waves produced are slightly different. Because the two sounds travel through the air at the same speed, their frequencies will be different as well. Consequently, sometimes the peaks of the waves will coincide. When this occurs, the sound of the two instruments together will be slightly louder than average. When the peak of one waveform coincides with the trough of another, the two will partially cancel each other out and the two instruments will sound slightly quieter than average. This is the phenomenon of interference. Notice that by itself each instrument—or each string of the same instrument—produces a steady tone. The wah-wah-wah effect that is easy to hear is a product of the interference of one source of sound with the other.

Waveforms have another property that must sometimes be considered in their description, namely their *phase.* If two waveforms with identical amplitudes and identical wavelengths are drawn on the same piece of graph paper, they may still fail to "line up" with each other because they may still differ in their phase, which is another way of saying that they are not in step with each other. Imagine that two waves that differ only in phase are made of stiff wire. It is easy to see that one wave may be pushed parallel to itself in either direction until the crests of both waves coincide. Under these conditions, the waves will add together with the result that the amplitude of the resulting wave will be twice as large as the component waves. Alternatively, one wave may be pushed parallel to itself until the crest of one wave coincides with the trough of another. The result is that the two waves cancel each other out completely. A simple waveform is completely identified when its amplitude, wavelength, and phase are specified. When the amplitude, wavelength, and phase of two simple waveforms are known, then it is possible to predict precisely how the two waves will interfere with each other.

Scientists have devised many clever experiments that demonstrate the way that light waves interfere with one another. (And notice that the property of interference demonstrates that light is a wave. By contrast, two solid bodies, whether they are two airplanes or a bat and a ball, cannot occupy the same volume of space at the same time. They cannot interfere with each other in the sense described above.) Many of these wave experiments—and some are performed with sound waves, some with water waves, and some with light waves—are variations of the following light experiment: Light from two identical light sources are shown on the same surface. Where crests coincide, the light on the surface is brighter, and where a trough and a crest combine, they cancel each other out to produce an unilluminated point on the surface. The resulting regular pattern of light and dark areas on the surface demonstrates how the two waves interfere with each other.

It is a distinguishing property of laser light that lasers can be created to shine at one particular wavelength. In other words, all of the energy of the laser is concentrated at a single frequency, and all of the light waves are in phase. To understand how this is accomplished, however, it is necessary to understand a little about the nature of light as a stream of particles.

The Particle Nature of Light

Atoms are the building blocks of the material world. There are roughly 100 different kinds of atoms—that is, there are approximately 100 different elements—and all gases, liquids, and solids are composed of various combinations and quantities of these atoms. Because atoms are so important, and because they are so small that they cannot be observed directly, scientists have spent a good deal of time developing models of atoms to assist them in visualizing their (atomic) properties.

About 100 years ago, scientists visualized atoms as tiny solar systems. It is an attractive analogy because there are several similarities between the two systems. Atoms consist mostly of empty space just as the solar system consists mostly of empty space. Most of the mass of the solar system is concentrated at its center in the body of the Sun, and similarly, most of the mass of an atom is concentrated at its center, called the nucleus, in the form of even smaller bodies called protons and neutrons. By ordinary standards, protons and neutrons are not very massive at all. One proton has a mass of approximately 1.67×10^{-27}kilograms, which is another way of saying that it takes almost 600,000,000,000,000,000,000,000,000 protons to equal one kilogram. Neutrons are approximately as massive as protons. All the protons and

Isaac Newton (1643–1727), English physicist and mathematician, founded the particle theory of light. [Library of Congress, Prints and Photographs Division]

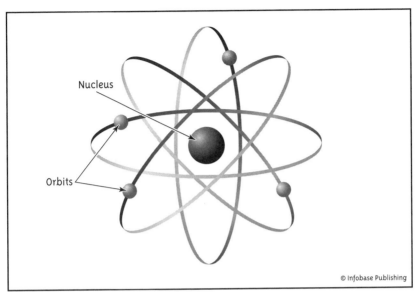

An earlier conception of the atom as a solar system in miniature.

neutrons that make up the atom are found within its nucleus. They are packed into what, even by atomic standards, is a very small volume of space. But while a proton may not be very massive compared to, say, an apple, it is very massive compared to the third and final component of every atom, the electron: A proton is 1,836 times as massive as an electron, and as the planets of the solar system orbit the Sun, the central mass of the solar system, all of an atom's electrons move about its nucleus. And so these early atomic scientists had a very convenient way of modeling an atom: They visualized each atom as a solar system in miniature.

But as with any analogy, this one also has its limitations. In the solar system, there is no reason why a planet, asteroid, comet, or spacecraft cannot orbit the Sun at any given distance. Provided a body has the necessary velocity and initial trajectory, it can and will orbit the Sun at any prescribed distance. In fact, NASA, the National Aeronautics and Space Administration, has become quite adept at placing spacecraft in orbit about the Sun at any prescribed distance. By contrast, scientists discovered early in their research that a model that assumed that electrons could orbit the nucleus in a more or less arbitrary manner did not agree with the experimental data; something was wrong with their model. Soon after discovering this shortcoming in the model, the Danish physicist Niels Bohr (1885–1962) hypothesized that electrons may only occupy certain specific regions, which are occasionally still called orbits, *and that each orbit represented a specific energy level for the atom.*

The assertion that there are only specific orbits and that each orbit represents a particular energy level for the atom is crucial in the study of lasers, because unlike planets, which remain in their orbits indefinitely, electrons can and often do change energy levels. These energy transitions may occur naturally, or they may occur as the result of human intervention. When the electrons associated with a particular atom are in their least energetic state, the atom to which they belong is said to be in ground state. When the atom absorbs energy, it moves into a higher energy state. The change in energy level occurs when an electron moves from a lower into a higher energy level. But because only specific energy levels are possible, the atom may absorb only specific quantities of energy. If a quantum of energy is exactly the amount needed for the atom to make the transition from one energy level to other, the atom may absorb the quantum of energy and make the transition to a higher energy state. If, on the another hand, the quantum of energy does not correspond to the precise amount necessary for the atom to make the transition from one energy level to another, the atom cannot absorb that energy packet. In other words, an atom may not absorb arbitrary amounts of energy. Instead, it may only absorb energy in certain specific amounts, where the precise amounts of energy that may be absorbed depend on the properties of that particular atom. The process of absorbing energy and moving from a lower to a higher energy state can be reversed. Exactly the same statements can be made about "excited" atoms—that is, atoms occupying energy states higher than the ground state—giving off certain discrete amounts of electromagnetic energy as they drop back down to lower energy states.

What does this have to do with light? The discrete packets of energy that atoms absorb or emit as they make transitions from lower to higher energy states and back down to lower energy states can sometimes be observed as *photons,* units of electromagnetic radiation that, when they exist at the right frequency, are visible as light. It is important to keep in mind that the precise wavelengths of electromagnetic radiation that an atom may absorb or emit depend upon the atom under consideration. Different types of atoms emit photons at different wavelengths.

Energy transitions can occur extremely quickly. An atom may jump to an excited state (by absorbing a photon) and back to the ground state (by emitting a photon) in a few 100 millionths of a second. The emission of a photon as the electron jumps back to ground state is called a *spontaneous emission.* An arbitrary collection of atoms that produces light via spontaneous emission will generally produce light in a variety of wavelengths and phases. Such a mixture of frequencies is called incoherent light. Sunlight is an example of incoherent light.

There is one more aspect of the absorption and emission of electromagnetic radiation that is important to this description of lasers. It is called *stimulated emission*, and inducing this phenomenon is crucial to the creation of laser light. Suppose that an atom is in a higher energy state (higher relative to the ground state) and that light of a particular wavelength—the "particular" wavelength depends on the atom—impinges on the excited atom. Under these conditions, the atom will be "stimulated" to emit a photon that is identical in wavelength and phase to the original photon. This effectively amplifies the initial photon, because "one went in and two came out." This phenomenon is unlikely to occur if the atom is only in the excited state for a hundred millionth of a second or so before dropping back to the ground state. In certain materials under certain conditions, however, another pathway back to the ground state exists, and this pathway is of great importance to the study of lasers.

Recall that in the phenomenon of spontaneous emission the atom jumps up to a higher energy level and then in a single step emits a photon and drops back down to ground level. For certain materials under certain conditions, however, the process of returning to ground level involves two steps. The atom passes through what is called a *metastable state*, a state that is very different from the high energy state that preceded it. The metastable state displays the following two properties: First, it is an energy level that is intermediate between the preceding higher energy level and the still lower ground state. Second, it is stable in the sense that an atom in a metastable state may remain in this state for a millisecond or even as long as a half-second. Compared to the time intervals to which humans are accustomed this is, of course, not long at all, but it is millions of times longer than the atom remained in the higher energy state and so the metastable state is, by comparison, very stable indeed.

From the point of view of lasers, the metastable state has one more property, and it is this property that makes the metastable state so important to the creation of laser light: When a photon of precisely the right energy interacts with the atom in this state, it will also emit a photon that is identical in wavelength to the photon that impinged upon it. Furthermore, because the atom can remain in a metastable state for what is, by atomic standards at least, a very long time, it is much more likely that a photon will impinge upon it while it is in this state.

The prediction of the existence of the phenomenon of stimulated emission was made by the physicist Albert Einstein (1879–1955), a prediction of which he was very proud. The experimental verification of the existence of the phenomenon was made not long after the initial prediction, but early experiments indicated that stimulated emission was very rare compared with spontaneous emission. Consequently, incoherent light seemed to be the natural state of affairs, and the production of coherent light, light waves that were of the same wavelength and in phase, seemed to be so unlikely as to be impossible. In fact, some physicists said exactly that. It would be decades before scientists and engineers learned to use the phenomenon of stimulated emission to produce regular bursts of light that consisted of precisely one wavelength; these were the first lasers. (As for Einstein, he did not live long enough to see his discovery of the phenomenon of spontaneous emission put to use in the first laser.) But once scientists and engineers discovered how to produce laser light using one material, they quickly discovered how to produce a wide variety of lasers of different wavelengths and levels of power.

Finally, for molecules, which consist of assemblages of atoms, there are other ways to raise the energy of the molecule from its ground state than the one already described. Collisions, for example, can cause the molecule to vibrate in certain very specific ways. These vibrations raise the energy level of the molecule above its ground state, and when dropping back to the ground state these molecules will emit photons at certain characteristic energies or frequencies. Scientists have also learned to make use of molecules in the production of laser light, and today lasers that exploit the vibrational energy of certain molecules are very common.

THE NATURE OF LASER LIGHT

L aser light is now used at supermarket checkouts, in CD and DVD players, in some toys (laser tag, for example), and to open some doors automatically, to name a few common applications. Newspapers and magazines carry occasional articles describing how lasers are used to track the motions of Earth's crust along the San Andreas Fault, to measure the Earth/Moon distance, and to shoot down airplanes and rockets. Other types of light are ill-suited for these applications, and so this raises the question: What makes laser light special? The answer is not as obvious as it might first appear. Although most of the lasers that one might see at the store, library, or hospital are red, lasers have been created in a variety of colors, and some very powerful lasers are invisible. While most people associate lasers with narrow beams of light, lasers can be made to simply glow softly. In fact, there are lasers from which laser light streams equally in all directions. Understanding what distinguishes laser light from other forms of light is necessary in order to appreciate what it is that makes lasers so special.

It is important to bear in mind that the same descriptive words—*wavelength, frequency, amplitude,* and *phase,* for example—that were used to describe light and other *electromagnetic waves* in the previous chapter are also used to describe light produced by lasers. Laser light shares

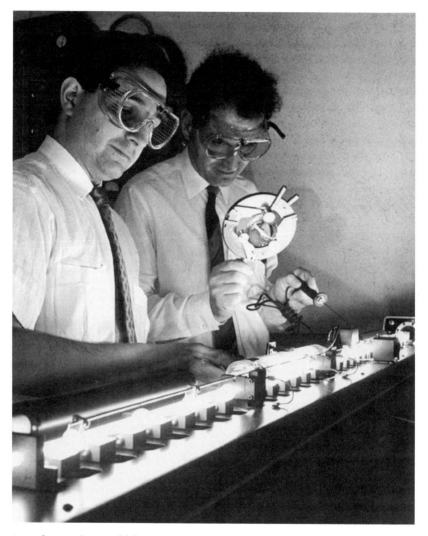

An early experiment with lasers at NASA's Electronics Resource Center. As many research-based organizations did, NASA quickly recognized the great potential of lasers to solve problems. [NASA]

many properties with sunlight and the light from incandescent bulbs. Laser light can even be a naturally occurring phenomenon. Under certain conditions, regions in the upper atmosphere of Mars spontaneously produce laser light. Given its many commonalities with other types of light, what makes laser light special?

Monochromatic Light

When sunlight is passed through a prism, it spreads out into its component colors and forms a rainbow. The pattern of colors that appears as the light emerges from the prism demonstrates that many different colors of light combine to form sunlight. This much is well known. Essentially the same thing, however, can be done with many other sources of light and with essentially the same result. (The rainbow effect is often harder to observe for other light sources because the light that enters the prism is often too weak to produce a bright rainbow as it emerges.) Nevertheless, most light sources, whether they are incandescent bulbs or stars, are composed of many different colors of light. The precise mix of colors present in each light source and the intensity of each color depend very much on how the light was produced. As a consequence, different light sources generally produce different rainbows, and each rainbow reveals a great deal about the source of light from which it came. Because the human eye perceives different frequencies of light waves as different colors—and because frequencies and wavelengths are closely related—the rainbow also reveals information about the wavelengths of light that are present in any given source.

Light produced by many lasers, however, is *monochromatic*—that is, if laser light is passed through a prism, the light that emerges will look exactly like the light that entered. If a beam of red laser light entered a prism, for example, a beam of red light will emerge. The "rainbow" consists of exactly one color. (Scientists have also learned how to create lasers that shine light at two, or even a few, colors, but these refinements will not be discussed here.) In other words, the form of light produced by a laser is extremely simple and regular. It can be visualized as the wave in the illustration in chapter 1, where a wave is depicted as a series of regularly spaced crests and troughs. Because the wave is so simple-looking, it makes sense to describe it in terms of its wavelength (or in terms of its frequency). Because the wavelength of visible light is so short, scientists often describe it in terms of nanometers. One nanometer is one billionth of a meter. While this is a convenient vocabulary to describe laser light, it makes no sense to talk about the frequency of sunlight, for example, because sunlight is composed of light waves of many different frequencies.

Whether laser light is described in terms of its color or its wavelength may not seem to matter. Because the human eye perceives

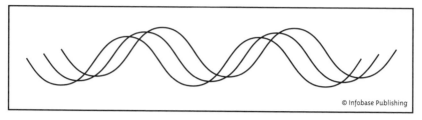

© Infobase Publishing

All three waves in the set have identical wavelengths and amplitudes, but their peaks occur in different locations.

different wavelengths as different colors, the two descriptions may seem equivalent, but there are two reasons that it is better to categorize laser light by wavelength (or frequency) rather than color. First, not all laser light is visible. Many common lasers "shine" at wavelengths that cannot be perceived by the human eye. Some of the lasers created for use in the operating room, for example, cannot be seen. The electromagnetic waves emanating from these lasers have wavelengths that are somewhat longer than those of red light, and the light waves that we perceive as red are the longest electromagnetic waves visible to the unaided eye. Their effects are visible, but the laser beams are not. While it makes no sense to describe the "color" of invisible electromagnetic waves, it makes perfect sense to describe these waves in terms of their wavelengths.

Second, describing light in terms of its component wavelengths enables one to be more precise. The human eye is not sensitive enough to distinguish two monochromatic light sources that have nearly identical wavelengths. Such lights are not the same, but they may well look the same. A wavelength description allows the observer to distinguish between two different but identical-looking waves.

Coherence

Laser light is extremely organized, exhibiting levels of organization that go beyond the mere fact that laser light consists of a single frequency. Such a high level of organization is very unusual in nature, and it is the reason that lasers have proven so useful. Imagine the light emanating from a laser as a large collection of individual waves. While the preceding section describes how all of the waves in the collection have identical wavelengths, there are many ways that such collection can be organized in space. In order to see what this means, imagine a collection of thin wires, and imagine that each wire is bent into a series of identical, regularly occurring, wavelike shapes. Imagine further

This laser emits its beam in the ultraviolet. It was one of the first commercially available lasers to emit its energy in that part of the electromagnetic spectrum. [Mary Evans Picture Library/The Image Works]

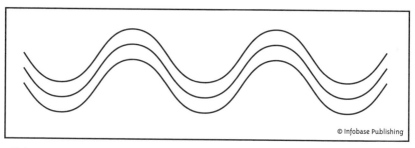

All three waves have identical wavelengths and amplitudes. They form a coherent set in the sense that their peaks occur at the same locations.

that the waves depicted by the wires have identical wavelengths, and for simplicity, imagine that they also have identical amplitudes. The wires can be placed on a flat surface in many ways. They could simply be tossed upon a table, in which case the "pattern" that they formed would be called incoherent. Alternatively, they could be rearranged in increasingly coherent patterns, but the most organized way to arrange the wires would be to place them so that their crests coincide. When light waves are organized in space so that their crests coincide, the light is said to be *coherent*. Again, by way of comparison, most naturally occurring light is not coherent, but laser light is extremely coherent.

Coherence is an important property because of the way that waves interact. Recall from chapter 1 that unlike wires, different waves can occupy the same volume of space at the same time. When waves occupy the same space at the same time, they combine to form a new wave, called the resultant wave, whose form is the sum of the individual waves. If the waves are incoherent, that is, if the crests and troughs are not lined up with one another, then cancellation can occur—wave crests may combine with wave troughs—and the resultant wave may be weaker than the component waves. Alternatively, suppose the troughs of each wave coincide with all the others; then the amplitude of the resultant wave will exceed the amplitude of the component waves, and in the process a brighter light is created. This is exactly what happens with laser light: The component waves are in phase with one another, and one consequence of this high degree of coherence is that light from lasers is intense.

Coherence in laser light occurs because of the phenomenon of *stimulated emission*. Recall from chapter 1 that stimulated emission occurs when an atom is in a higher energy state and a passing *photon* stimulates that excited atom to emit a photon of its own. (As it emits this photon, the atom takes the transition down to a lower, more stable energy level.) The new photon obtained as a result of this process begins its journey in phase with the photon that caused it to be emitted. Because these photons then continue to stimulate the emission of other photons—assuming that everything is working right—the result is a very large number of photons all of which exhibit identical frequencies. Laser light may retain its coherence over distances measured in kilometers, which, given the extremely short wavelengths involved, is remarkable. Eventually, however, its coherence degrades.

There is still another ordered geometric property that most lasers exhibit. The collection of individual waves of which a laser beam is composed travel paths that are nearly parallel with one another. This is what makes a laser beam "beamlike," that is, tightly focused over long distances. It may seem as if this is a necessary result of coherence, but it is actually a separate property. To create the beam, the laser must be designed with the beam in mind. Some lasers produce beams that are tightly focused over distances of hundreds or even thousands of kilometers. Some lasers lose their focus much sooner. The laser beam, contrary to popular belief, is not an intrinsic aspect of laser light.

The confusion results in part from the way that light waves are depicted on paper. The "waveform" found in chapter 1, could be drawn by a pencil. The pencil creates a dot on the paper, and then as the pencil point is moved up and down and to the right, the result is a "sinusoidal" waveform, a curve. It is a useful model because it illustrates the concepts of amplitude, phase, and wavelength, but as a model it has its limitations. Real light waves form a wave front, or surface, that passes through space in a way that is somewhat similar to the way that the membrane of a balloon expands and stretches as the balloon is inflated.

A wave front expanding through three-dimensional space differs from the sinusoidal wave pictured in chapter 1 because the wave front quickly spreads out, and as it does so it becomes less intense. To see how this might work, first imagine dropping a stone in a quiet pool of water. This creates a circular wave that expands outward equally in all directions. Initially, in the region near the splash zone, the wave may be fairly large. All of the energy of the wave is evenly distributed along the small wave front. As the wave spreads out, its total energy remains the same because no additional energy is being added. The result is that the energy per unit length of the wave front diminishes, and the farther the wave spreads out, the less energy there is per unit length of wave front. This is an example of a wave moving along a (two-dimensional) surface.

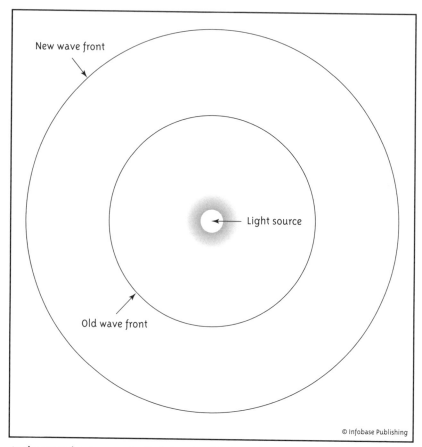

As the wave front expands, the intensity of light at the wave front diminishes as the inverse of the square of the distance to the source.

To see how a wave might expand outward into three-dimensional space, imagine a small (idealized) lightbulb positioned so that it shines in every direction equally. Imagine placing the tiny bulb at the center of a sphere of radius one meter. Suppose further that x units of light energy are streaming out of the bulb. (The units by which energy are measured do not matter for purposes of this discussion.) Because the light shines equally in all directions, the energy will be equally distributed all across the inside surface of the sphere. Recall that the surface area of a sphere of radius r meters is πr^2—the expression πr^2 is another way of writing $\pi \times r \times r$; and π is a number a little bigger than three—and so the formula for surface area indicates that the surface area of a sphere of radius one meter is π square meters. At the surface of this sphere, the light is shining with an intensity of x/π units of energy per square meter. Now consider the intensity of the light along the wave front when it has expanded into a sphere of radius two meters. This time the surface of the sphere has an area of 4π square meters, which is four times the area of a sphere of radius one meter. Consequently, the light energy produced by the tiny bulb has spread out over an area four times as large as was previously considered. The intensity of the light on the surface of the larger sphere, then, is $x/(4\pi)$ units per square meter. This shows that the intensity of the light emitted by the bulb deceases by a factor of four whenever the distance from the wave front to the bulb is increased by a factor of two. This explains why it is not possible to illuminate the Moon with a searchlight; light from a searchlight spreads out rapidly, much like the idealized small bulb, and so virtually all of the light emitted by the searchlight misses the Moon. Only the light that strikes the Moon can be reflected back toward Earth, but the light that reflects off the Moon is already extremely weak, and what little of this light reflects off the Moon in the direction of Earth continues to spread rapidly outward like waves in a pool. By the time the reflected light reaches Earth it is too weak to detect.

Lasers are different. They can be constructed so that the light rays that compose the laser beam are nearly parallel. The wave front for a laser beam is a tiny surface that remains tiny over large distances. Consequently, a laser beam is almost as intense at a distance of two meters, for example, as it is at a distance of one meter. In particular, the beam's wave front does not expand outward in space like the surface of a balloon, but instead moves forward as if it were the end of a pole or beam. This property leads to some unexpected results. For example, laser beams that shine in the visible part of the electromagnetic spectrum are nevertheless usually invisible until they strike a solid object. In order for something to be visible, light rays from that object must enter our eyes. Because the light waves that are emitted by lasers do not spread out, they do not enter our eyes until they strike an object and are reflected. Because most surfaces are uneven and rough, the reflected laser light spreads out and shines about the room. At this time it is simultaneously visible to individuals at different positions. Before the laser strikes an object, however, the light does not enter the observer's eyes because the beam does not spread out. (One must always be careful to *never* look into a laser beam, because the light from even a weak laser is generally intense enough to cause permanent and severe eye damage.)

Throughout this book, there are photographs that show laser beams. These were made using various tricks to make the beams visible. For example, smoke can be blown across a laser beam, and the particles in the smoke will scatter some of the laser light about the room (and in particular toward the lens of the camera), causing it to become visible. But without the smoke, laser light beams remain invisible until they strike something.

The Concept of Laser Power and Efficiency

In every discussion of lasers, extraordinary claims are made about laser power, but without a clear understanding of what power is, it is hard to know what these claims mean. To understand the claims, it is important to first understand the concept of *work*.

This is the target chamber of the National Ignition Facility, a 1-million-pound, 10-meter-diameter aluminum sphere that functions as the interface between a target, high-energy lasers, and numerous measurement devices. The laser system can produce a pulse equal in power to 1,000 times the electric generating power of the United States. [U.S. Department of Energy]

Energy is often described as the capacity for doing work. Early in the history of science, mechanical energy, sometimes defined as the ability to raise a weight, was considered to be different from thermal energy, which shows up as a change in the temperature of a body. This perception was abandoned during the 19th century. This was the Age of Steam, a time when engineers were busy designing and constructing steam engines whose purpose was to turn heat energy into mechanical energy. As scientists and engineers struggled to discover the principles by which these machines were governed, and as they sought to discover the limitations of this type of technology, they made one of the great scientific discoveries of the 19th century: Mechanical energy and thermal energy are two forms of the same quantity. One can convert mechanical energy into thermal energy and thermal energy into mechanical energy. For example, friction is the conversion of mechanical energy into thermal energy. One can also convert thermal energy into mechanical energy, and this is exactly what the steam engine does—the automobile engine and the aircraft engine too. As a consequence, scientists and engineers now use one unit of measurement to describe both mechanical and thermal energy. Today, all energy is measured in terms of the *joule*. One joule (1 J) is defined as the work done by exerting a force of one newton over a distance of one meter. (One newton (1 N) equals about 0.22 pounds.) Alternatively, 4.184 J is the amount of heat energy that must be supplied to raise the temperature of one gram of water by one degree Celsius at atmospheric pressure. (This amount of thermal energy is also known as a calorie; therefore, 4.184 J equals one calorie.) In describing the amount of energy delivered to a target by a laser, the quantity of energy is described in terms of joules.

Knowing that work was performed or that heat was supplied to a target, however, does not tell the whole story. Work can be performed at different rates. A one-newton bag of pennies can be raised a distance of one meter by raising one penny each minute until the bag is empty (and then lifting the empty bag), or the entire bag can be lifted a distance of one meter over the course of one minute. The first method takes a lot longer than the second—about 360 times as long—but the same amount of work is performed in each case, because the same weight is moved over the same distance.

To quantify the rate at which work is performed requires the concept of *power*. Power is the amount of work performed per unit of time. In science, power is usually measured in terms of *watts*. One watt equals one joule per second. Notice that it is possible to use watts to describe the rate at which the bag of pennies described earlier can be raised. One simply divides the number of joules expended in raising the pennies one meter—it is 1 J—by the amount of time elapsed from start to finish. If it takes 360 times as long to raise the pennies one at a time at a rate of one per minute than to raise the bag over the course of one minute, then the power needed to raise them one by one is only 1/360th that required to raise them together. This is comparatively easy to see when considering the question of raising a weight, but one can employ exactly the same concepts to describe the rate at which water is heated. A heat source capable of producing 4.184 watts will raise the temperature of one gram of water by one degree Celsius in one second. By contrast, a source need only produce 0.06973 watts (0.06973 = 4.148 ÷ 60) continuously over a period of one minute (60 seconds) to raise the temperature of the same amount of water by one degree Celsius.

Why is this so important for understanding lasers? There are lasers that can produce billions or even trillions of watts of power, and it is natural to ask, how is this possible? Part of the answer lies in the definition of a watt. Recall that the watt is a *ratio* between the amount of work done (measured in joules) and the amount of time elapsed between the beginning and end of the process. A laser that can produce 1 J in 1/100 of a second—recall that 1 J is not nearly enough to raise the temperature of one gram of water one degree Celsius—has produced 100 watts of power during that hundredth of a second. If that same laser can deliver that same joule in 1/10,000th of a second, it has produced 10,000 watts. Now suppose that the 100-watt laser described in the preceding sentence is a pulsed laser, that is, it operates only for short periods of time. (Pulsed lasers are a very common type of laser.) For purposes of illustration, suppose that the laser operates only for one second out of every minute—in other words, it emits a pulse for one second and is off for the next 59 seconds. The definition of a watt means that while the laser was working, it produced 100 watts of power. This is called its peak power. Its average power, measured over the course of one minute, is much lower because for much of the time the laser produced no power whatsoever. Claims about the amount of power produced by a laser must be treated with care.

Finally, there is one more important consideration in discussing lasers: the concept of efficiency. Lasers require an outside power source to produce their light. In the process of producing laser light, lasers consume electrical energy, which, of course, is also measured in watts. In fact, it is sometimes convenient to think of lasers as energy consumers rather than as producers, because lasers generally consume more electrical energy than they produce in the form of a beam of laser light. The difference between the amount of energy the laser consumes and the amount it produces in the form of a beam of light is wasted energy. Some of the electrical energy, for example, is converted into heat energy. Some of the electrical energy is converted into laser light that "leaks" out the side of the tube where the laser light is generated. This light is not incorporated into the beam so it, too, is wasted. The less electrical energy is wasted, the more efficient the laser is.

Scientists and engineers represent the idea of *efficiency* with a fraction. The numerator of the fraction is the amount of energy produced by the laser in the form of a beam of laser light. The denominator of the fraction is the amount of electrical energy consumed by the laser, and the result is multiplied by 100 percent:

$$\textit{efficiency} = \frac{\textit{light energy produced}}{\textit{electrical energy consumed}} \times 100\%$$

A perfectly efficient laser would simply convert all of the electrical energy it consumed into a beam of laser light. That is 100 percent efficiency, and that never happens. In practice, lasers generally operate at less than 50 percent efficiency. Often they operate at efficiencies of much less than 50 percent. Why this is so can be seen by examining the very first laser.

3

CREATING
LASER LIGHT

American physicist Theodore Maiman (1927–   ) built the first working laser in 1960. At the time, Maiman was working at the Hughes Research Laboratories. He had already studied the *maser*, a recently invented device that is, in principle, similar to a laser but produces coherent, focused microwaves rather than light waves (masers are described in chapter 5). In fact, he discovered ways to improve masers. His work with microwaves, *electromagnetic waves* with wavelengths somewhat longer than visible light, led him to attempt to create a device similar to a maser that would emit coherent, focused light, a device that was originally called an optical maser but is today known as a laser. Although Maiman worked largely alone at Hughes Research, he was not the only person to believe that the laser was possible. Others were working on the problem as well. Maiman was simply the first to overcome the technical hurdles involved. Maiman's solution to these fundamental problems was the ruby laser. It is a perfect illustration of the basic physical principles described in the preceding chapters, and it is well worth the time to examine Maiman's device in some detail.

Laser experiment at the Idaho National Engineering and Environmental Laboratory. While the basic principles by which lasers shine remain unchanged, new applications for lasers as well as new laser designs are continually being discovered. [U.S. Department of Energy]

Stimulated Emission

The first problem Maiman had to overcome was to find a way to produce coherent light.

Recall that an atom, when excited by light of a particular frequency, will make the transition to a higher *energy level*. Once in the higher energy level, however, it spontaneously makes the transition back to *ground state* and in the process emits a *photon*. As a general rule, most atoms spend so little time in the higher energy state that it is very unlikely that the phenomenon of *stimulated emission* (described in chapter 1) will occur, and without stimulated emission, laser light cannot occur, because it is only through stimulated emission, not *spontaneous emission*, that coherent light is generated. This was the first problem Maiman had to solve.

Maiman's goal, therefore, was to create a situation that scientists describe as a *population inversion*. To understand what is meant by the term, keep in mind that most of the time the ground state is the normal state for an atom. In other words, under normal conditions most atoms in a population of atoms are in the ground state most of the time. (Here the word *population* is used as a synonym for set.) Normally, only a few atoms are in a higher energy state at any given instant. Maiman had to invert the normal scheme of things and create conditions in which many atoms were simultaneously in a higher energy state, that is, he had to create conditions in which a higher energy state became a new normal state. Nor was that enough. He had to find a way to maintain the atoms in that higher energy state long enough so that stimulated emission could occur. This is the state that scientists call a population inversion. Under these conditions, many atoms can simultaneously become involved in the phenomenon of stimulated emission: As one atom emits a photon, another atom is stimulated to emit a photon that is in phase and at the same wavelength as the previously emitted photon. These two photons stimulate the emission of two more. These four stimulate the emission of four more, and so on.

The key to obtaining a population inversion is to create a longer-lasting, higher energy state, called a *metastable state*, in a majority of the atoms. Several materials were available. Maiman decided to use chromium atoms. Chromium atoms absorb light and jump to a high energy level. They remain there very briefly, and then drop to a metastable state, which is a higher energy level than the ground state but lower than the so-called high energy state that immediately preceded it. Undisturbed, they can remain in the metastable state for what, by atomic standards, is a very long time. (In this case, the metastable state is only a fraction of a second, but it is millions of times longer than the atom can maintain the initial high energy state.) By bombarding chromium atoms with the right frequencies of light, Maiman hoped that many of the atoms would transition from the ground to the metastable state by way of the high energy state, and from the metastable state, he wanted them to partici-pate in the phenomenon of stimulated emission.

The element chromium is, however, a gray metal, impervious to light and not of much use by itself. (None of the atoms inside a bar of chromium, for example, can be exposed to light, and the photons emit-ted by the surface atoms generally travel outward and so encounter no additional chromium atoms.) Maiman's solution was to use a ruby rather than a piece of pure chromium. The reason is that light passes easily through a ruby crystal, and the red color of the gem is due to the presence of chromium atoms. Naturally occurring rubies are full of impurities that make them unsuitable for the type of application

Maiman had in mind. Instead he chose a synthetic ruby, a cylindrical pink crystal with a carefully controlled chemical composition. (It bears little resemblance to what one finds in a piece of jewelry.) Essentially, the ruby allowed him to expose the chromium atoms *inside* the crystal to light. The crystal was simply a transparent medium that held the chromium atoms in place in a latticelike structure so that they could be raised into the metastable state.

Chromium atoms absorb light in the blue and green region of the *spectrum*. This causes them to make a brief transition to a higher energy level. At this point, they transition to the metastable state. Left to themselves, these atoms will eventually and spontaneously emit the necessary photon that makes it possible for them to return to ground state. But when one of these atoms emits a photon and makes the transition back to the ground state, and if a neighboring atom is also in the metastable state, and if the photon is emitted in the right direction, the emitted photon may interact with the other atom that is still in the metastable state and cause the phenomenon of stimulated emission: Another photon is produced that is identical in *frequency* and *phase* with the initial photon. It is the energy of the photon emitted during this process, rather than the pink color of the ruby, that accounts for the red light that is characteristic of ruby lasers.

To get the process started, Maiman placed the ruby crystal at the center of a helical lamp. This ensured that the crystal would be bombarded with light. The exact characteristics of the light were not important. (Recall that most light is a rich mix of *wavelengths*.) All that was necessary was to choose a lamp with two properties. First, in addition to whatever other wavelengths emanated from the lamp, it had to produce light at a wavelength of 550 nanometers, which is the wavelength necessary to excite the chromium atoms into making the initial transition. Second, the light had to be very bright, because the goal was to raise the energy level of most of the chromium atoms—a population inversion—and without sufficient energy the population inversion cannot occur. Maiman accomplished both of these goals by using a xenon flash lamp, which was a popular light for high-speed photography. It produces a brilliant, if brief, burst of light. The term *brief* is, however, a relative term. By human standards the flash was brief—less than a second—but because everything connected with light happens so quickly, the flash was long enough to bring the process of producing a laser beam to a conclusion. To produce the laser beam again, one lights the lamp again. Maiman's ruby laser is an example of a pulsed laser because the beam is produced in brief pulses. It is also possible to design continuous wave, or CW, lasers, devices that produce an uninterrupted laser beam. (The most common type of CW laser is described in chapter 6.)

The Laser Beam

There is nothing in the phenomenon of stimulated emission that requires the light so produced to shine in a particular direction. With respect to Maiman's ruby laser, light "leaked" out of the crystal in all directions. Had he not further altered the ruby, he would only have been successful in producing a momentary glow emanating at a single (red) wavelength. The result would be a laser glow rather than a laser beam. There is more involved in the production of a laser beam than the production of laser light.

Because the photons produced in a ruby by stimulated emission are emitted in all directions, Maiman knew that some had to be emitted parallel to the axis of symmetry of the ruby. (The axis of symmetry of the ruby is the centerline of the ruby rod.) Maiman's next design problem involved using the photons that traveled along the crystal's axis of symmetry to force the ruby to shine preferentially in that direction. He

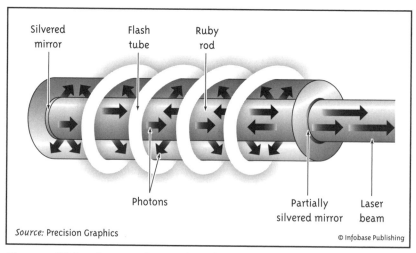

Source: Precision Graphics

© Infobase Publishing

Diagram of Maiman's conception. A ruby rod provides the lasing medium. The chromium atoms are pumped, or excited, by the helical flash lamp, and a population inversion is created. A laser beam is formed as photons resonate between the two mirrors. From the partially silvered end of the rod emerges the beam.

did this by amplifying the light that traveled along the crystal's axis and ignoring the light that leaked out the sides of the crystal. Amplification, it turns out, can be achieved most simply by using mirrors.

The first step in amplifying the light emitted by the chromium atoms was to make sure that the ends of the rod satisfied the following criteria: (1) They had to be as flat as possible, and (2) they had to be perpendicular to the rod's axis of symmetry. Two flat surfaces that are perpendicular to the same line are parallel to each other. Consequently, the ruby rod had flat, parallel ends.

Next, Maiman coated the ends of the crystal so that they would act as mirrors. As photons traveled the length of the crystal (at the speed of light in the crystal), they encountered additional chromium atoms in a metastable state. Additional photons were produced via the process of stimulated emission. Almost immediately, a stream of photons reached the end of the rod, where they were reflected back into the crystal to repeat the process. Photons that were emitted in a direction parallel to the rod's axis of symmetry became trapped inside the crystal, "bouncing" back and forth from one end of the rod to the other. These trapped photons quickly increased in number, and in this way a relative handful of photons were amplified to produce a powerful beam of light that continued to be reflected back and forth from one end of the crystal to the other.

Notice that the assertion that light "continues to be reflected back and forth from one end of the crystal to the other" indicates that our description of Maiman's laser cannot be complete. Confining the beam to the inside of the crystal may make for an interesting laboratory experiment, but it fails to produce a usable laser beam. In order to make the laser work, the beam has to get out of the crystal. The solution to the problem of the confined beam is to make one of the mirrors a little less than opaque. In other words, while one mirror will reflect back into the crystal all of the light that impinges upon it, the second mirror will reflect only some (but not all) of the light. The rest of the light escapes through this second mirror, and it is this light that constitutes the laser beam.

Most of the light that eventually exits from the less reflective end of the rod will make multiple trips, back and forth, along the length of the laser cavity before it escapes. (The technical term for this regular back and forth motion is *oscillation*.) In particular, if a photon is not traveling a path that is almost exactly parallel to the axis of symmetry of the rod, it will exit the side of the rod rather than the end. This is why the geometry of the crystal is critical: The right geometry guarantees

The Tacoma Narrows Bridge, November 7, 1940, a famous example of the phenomenon of resonance. The wind caused the bridge to begin to oscillate. Continued wind
caused the amplitude of the oscillations to slowly increase until they tore the bridge
apart. [Topham/The Image Works]

that the light waves escaping from the less reflective end are almost
perfectly parallel, which explains why the beam that emanates from the
end remains focused over long distances. (In many later lasers, the light
is further concentrated by using one or more lenses.)

The phenomenon that occurs inside the crystal rod as light *oscillates*
from one end to the other with increasing intensity is called *resonance*.
The resonance effect is extremely important in many aspects of engineering, both mechanical and electrical. The most famous example of
uncontrolled resonance in the field of mechanical engineering occurred
in the destruction in November 1940 of the Tacoma Narrows Bridge
in Washington State. Shortly after the bridge was completed, a strong,
steady wind set the deck of the bridge oscillating. The oscillations
were gentle at first—just as the amplification of laser light is modest at
first—but over time the bridge oscillations increased in amplitude until
the bridge was destroyed. Similarly, continued oscillations inside the
crystal increase the strength of the beam, but in the case of a laser, the

oscillations soon produce a steady beam of light whose strength remains constant. By contrast with the bridge, the resonance that occurs within the ruby is there by design. Finally, unlike the bridge oscillations, which were extremely dramatic—many people find the film of the destruction of the bridge unforgettable—the oscillations that make lasers possible occur too quickly to see. Because they happen at the speed of light, most people are unaware that they occur at all.

The discovery that one could create resonance inside the crystal using such a simple technique was a conceptually elegant and technically important breakthrough. It enabled engineers to turn a laser glow into a laser beam. Maiman was not the first scientist to understand the principle, but he was the first to put it into practice in the creation of a laser.

All of the physical processes described in this section are summarized in the word *laser*, which is an acronym for "light amplification by stimulated emission of radiation." The preceding presentation explains in some detail the process of stimulated emission and how the light produced by that process is amplified by the design of Maiman's ruby crystal. All of the words comprising the acronym have now been defined, except the last. The word *radiation* refers to the fact that light was a form of electromagnetic radiation. The word *laser* was coined by the inventor of the device, Gordon Gould, in 1957; it is a new word for a new type of device.

The Ruby Laser

Maiman's invention worked as follows: The electrical power was turned on; the light flashed; the ruby was flooded with light, which quickly raised many of the chromium atoms into the metastable state; stimulated emission occurred; the light resonated inside the laser cavity; and from out of one end of the rod shone history's first laser beam at a wavelength of 694.3 nanometers. To better understand how this laser worked, it is important to examine how much of the electrical power that flowed into the flash lamp was converted into the laser beam and how much was wasted. In other words, how efficient was Maiman's laser? And, because Maiman's laser is still fairly typical of how most lasers work, how efficient is any laser?

Notice, first, that Maiman's laser required an outside power source. It is, in that sense, a conversion device: It converts electrical energy into a beam of coherent light, and it accomplishes this conversion via a series of steps. Three of these steps are extremely wasteful.

Early version of the ruby laser. The ruby was built inside an elliptical chamber that has been opened to reveal the ruby crystal and flash lamp. [SSPL/The Image Works]

First, as with every lamp, Maiman's xenon flash lamp exhibited resistance to the flow of electrical current. A more common example of the phenomenon of electrical resistance, one with which most people are familiar, is the ordinary incandescent bulb. Most of the electricity consumed by these bulbs is converted to heat, not light. In that sense, the heat is wasted energy. Maiman's lamp resisted the flow of electricity and in the process converted much of the electricity that flowed into it into heat rather than light.

Second, the light that emanated from Maiman's lamp consisted of many wavelengths. If the light from the bulb was passed through a prism, it would emerge as a rainbow. Recall that chromium atoms only respond to light in a very narrow part of the spectrum. To return to the rainbow of the preceding sentence, only a very small part of the rainbow is of any use in exciting the chromium atoms; none of the remaining wavelengths enable the chromium atoms to make the transition to higher energy states. No matter how long those other frequencies shine or how bright they are, they will not cause a population inversion in the chromium atoms.

The third source of loss is related to the geometry of the invention: Look back at the diagram of Maiman's laser on page 34. Most of the light that emanates from the lamp misses the ruby rod entirely. This is true for all parts of the electromagnetic spectrum produced by the lamp. Unless the light waves enter the ruby rod, they can have no effect on the chromium atoms within. Consequently, the light that failed to shine on the crystal was another source of loss. The electrical energy that was converted into the light that illuminated the walls, ceiling, and floor of the room, but not the crystal, was wasted energy. The result of these three processes is that most of the electrical energy that entered the lamp was converted into forms of energy that did not contribute to a population inversion, and much of the remaining energy, the light energy that could have contributed to a population inversion, failed to enter the ruby rod.

Finally, notice what happens to the light produced inside the rod by stimulated emission. It is impossible to control the direction that the photons are emitted. A few are initially emitted along the axis of symmetry of the rod, but many are not. Consequently, some of the light produced by stimulated emission shines—or "leaks," depending on one's point of view—through the side of the rod. This laser light does not contribute to the laser beam. This, too, is waste, and there is nothing to be done about it.

Maiman's famous 1960 paper, "Stimulated Optical Radiation in Ruby," in which he described his accomplishment, is only four brief paragraphs long, and it does not address the issue of how efficient is his original laser. (He was interested only in demonstrating that he had priority over the many other engineers and scientists who were hard at work attempting to create the first laser.) Ruby lasers, however, rarely reach efficiencies of more than a few percent. Some are less than 1 percent efficient. That is, only 1 percent of the energy that enters the device exits the device in the form of a laser beam. Since it is one of the great laws of physics that energy can neither be created nor destroyed, this means that the remaining 99 percent or so of the energy consumed by the laser is wasted in the sense that it contributes nothing to the beam. In particular, the conversion of electricity to heat is such a problem that some ruby lasers are water cooled.

Maiman's original design has been modified and improved in many ways over the intervening years, but the basic principles remain the same. To give some indication of the nature of these improvements, consider the problem of focusing the incoherent light source onto the ruby crystal. One way this is now done is to use an elliptical cylinder. Recall that an ellipse is a curve determined by two points, here represented by the letters f_1 and f_2, and a distance, usually represented by the letter r. (The points f_1 and f_2 are called the foci of the ellipse.) Now consider a point, P, on the plane. If the distance from P to f_1 plus the distance from P to f_2 equals r; then the point P is on the ellipse. If the sum of the distances is different from r then P is not part of the ellipse. See the illustration on the bottom of this page. If the ellipse is moved perpendicularly to the plane in which it was drawn, it traces a surface in space called an elliptical cylinder, a cylinder whose sides are perpendicular to its base and whose cross-sections, when taken parallel to the base, are ellipses. Notice that when this is done the foci of the original ellipse are drawn out into what are called the focal lines of the elliptical cylinder.

It is a property of an ellipse that a ray that lies in the plane of the ellipse and emanates from one of its foci will be reflected off the sides of the ellipse in such a way that it passes through the other focus. (One can experience this effect in the National Statuary Hall in Washington, D.C., which was designed as a whispering gallery. The shape of the room is half of an ellipsoid, a three-dimensional shape obtained from an ellipse by rotating the ellipse about one of its axes of symmetry. If one stands at one focus and whispers, the sound waves are reflected off the walls and ceilings and are concentrated at the other focus so that two

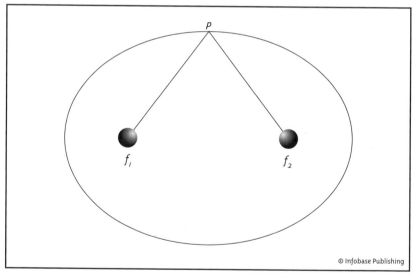

© Infobase Publishing

Given any point P on the ellipse, the sum of the distances from P to the two foci is the same. If one constructs a cylinder with the ellipse as base so that the sides of the cylinder are perpendicular to the base, one obtains an elliptical cylinder. The foci of the ellipse become the focal lines of the cylinder, and any ray emanating perpendicularly from a focal line will be reflected off the sides of the cylinder toward the other focal line.

people, one standing at each focus, can whisper to each other and hear each other's voices even though they are far from each other and in a room filled with people.) If, in the design of a laser, one uses an elliptical cylinder with a highly polished inner surface and places the ruby crystal along one focal line and a source of incoherent light along the other, one can obtain the same general effect: The light rays that emanate directly out from the incoherent source will reflect off the sides of the cylinder and converge on the crystal. As a consequence, one can induce the phenomenon of stimulated emission with less energy because more of the light emitted from the incoherent source is used in creating and maintaining the metastable state inside the crystal.

Finally, it is worth noting that although the laser is now described as one of the great inventions of the 20th century, its importance was not initially recognized. The journal *Nature*, for example, was not Maiman's first choice for a peer-reviewed publication. He originally submitted his paper, "Stimulated Optical Radiation in Ruby," to a scientific journal called *Physical Review*, and they rejected it because they thought it was too similar to another paper that Maiman had already published. But the earlier paper, which was concerned with a topic related to the creation of a ruby laser, did not describe the creation of a laser.

Even after the paper was published in a reputable scientific journal, many scientists still failed to see the value of Maiman's creation. They understood the principles used in its creation but not its potential usefulness. They were not alone. At the time of its invention, even many of the scientists involved in laser research could not have described how the device might be used to improve the lives of ordinary people. Nevertheless, few devices created in the last 50 years have had more of an impact on humans' lives than the laser.

4

THE EARLY HISTORY OF LASERS

Albert Einstein (1879–1955), German-American physicist, who discovered the phenomenon of stimulated emission [AAPL/HIP/The Image Works]

The early history of lasers begins with the German-American physicist Albert Einstein (1879–1955). In 1917 Einstein published a paper entitled "On the Quantum Theory of Radiation" describing the process of *stimulated emission* for the first time. Neither in this paper nor afterward did he suggest any applications that might evolve out of his efforts to understand light. He does not seem to have even considered the possibility that his work might have practical applications. A novel theoretical insight was enough for him, and there the matter rested for the next several decades. During this time, there were few experiments and no inventions employing the phenomenon of stimulated emission.

To be sure, physicists accepted the existence of stimulated emission as a phenomenon. In order for stimulated emission to be useful, however, one would have to achieve a population inversion, and many thought that the laws of thermodynamics made the creation of such a state impossible. Consequently, no one bothered investigating it further. Stimulated emission seemed an interesting but not especially useful aspect of nature. It was, they supposed, one of nature's little oddities. Virtually all of the light that had shown on Earth since the beginning of time was incoherent light. They concluded, therefore, that the coherent laser light with which we are now so familiar, was impossible to create.

Charles Hard Townes (1915–), American physicist and inventor of the maser [Topham/The Image Works]

After World War II, three physicists began working on the theoretical and practical problems of creating a device that would amplify electromagnetic radiation via the process of stimulated emission. Two of those physicists were from the Soviet Union, Aleksandr M. Prokharov (1916–2002) and Nikolay G. Basov (1922–2001). The third scientist was an American, Charles H. Townes (1915–). They received little encouragement. In fact, many of their colleagues actively discouraged them from continuing this line of research. In 2001, the year before his death, Prokharov told Russian state television that many of his fellow scientists thought that he and Basov were "crazy" to try to achieve something that was so obviously impossible. In the United States, Townes's colleagues asked that his funding be cut because he was simply wasting money. By the time of their request, Townes had already spent $30,000, a substantial amount of money at the time. Fortunately, neither Townes nor Prokharov and Basov were not easily discouraged, and in 1964 all three received the Nobel Prize for their work in this field.

The three physicists' work resulted in the creation of a device called a *maser*, an acronym for "microwave amplification by stimulated emission of radiation," a device that is similar in concept (as well as in name) to the laser. Townes was the first to create a maser. Recall that light consists of those wavelengths of electromagnetic radiation that are visible. When light waves impinge on the human retina, specialized structures on the retina, called rods and cones, emit nerve impulses that travel to the brain along the optic nerve, with the result that the observer sees those objects that reflected the light. By contrast, while microwaves may enter the eye, they do not have the same effect on the rods and cones. They are, as a consequence, invisible. Microwaves, which have wavelengths between 1 millimeter and 1 meter, are another small segment of the invisible part of the electromagnetic spectrum. Townes, Prokharov, and Basov discovered how to create a device based on the same general principles as a laser but that "shone" in the microwave part of the spectrum.

To create this device, these scientists had to overcome the same basic problems that Maiman later overcame. Townes was the first to construct a working maser. The first choice he had to make was to find a material that would emit microwaves via the process of stimulated emission. He chose ammonia gas—ammonia because it exhibited the phenomenon of stimulated emission in the microwave region of the spectrum and a gas because it enabled him to physically separate individual molecules in a way that was both efficient and relatively fast. (An ammonia molecule consists of one nitrogen and three hydrogen atoms.) Not surprisingly, Townes's maser was technically quite different from Maiman's laser.

By contrast with chromium atoms, which make the transition to a *metastable state* via a three-step process—*ground state* to higher state to metastable state—ammonia molecules experience only two states, a higher and lower one. Stimulated emission can be elicited from the higher energy state of the ammonia molecule provided one can create a population inversion.

Townes's approach to the creation of a population inversion was entirely different from that of Maiman. Whereas Maiman excited chromium atoms into a higher energy state by adding energy to the laser crystal via his xenon lamp, Townes made use of the fact that in any population of ammonia molecules at least a few of the molecules are already in the higher energy state. Under normal conditions, however, the higher energy molecules simply are not dense enough in the gas to enable the phenomenon of stimulated emission to occur. In order to facilitate the phenomenon of stimulated emission, Townes had to increase the percentage of molecules in the higher energy state. In other words, he had to create a population inversion. Townes achieved this by removing the molecules in the lower state and thereby creating a new population consisting largely of molecules in the higher energy state. Notice that he did not raise the energy level of any molecule but, instead, created a new population by separating out the higher energy molecules from the lower energy ones.

The key to this approach is that the electrical properties of the ammonia molecules in the ground state are different from those of ammonia molecules in the higher energy level. Townes made use of this fact by injecting ammonia gas into a chamber, called a focuser, in which he had created an electrical field. The way that the ammonia molecules interacted with the electrical field depended on their energy level. As the gas passed through this chamber, the molecules in the lower energy state were directed out of the stream. The remaining molecules, consisting of those in the higher energy state, were funneled by the electrical field into a chamber. In other words, he obtained a population inversion by retaining only those molecules already in the higher energy state.

The chamber in which the higher energy molecules were directed was designed so that the microwaves could reflect back and forth inside the chamber, creating a highly coherent, more powerful wave via the phenomenon of stimulated emission. In Townes's device, the emitted frequency of the resulting *electromagnetic wave* was approximately 24 gigahertz, which corresponds to a wavelength of approximately 1.25 centimeters. Like Maiman, Townes needed to find a way to get some of the resulting electromagnetic energy out of the resonator, but at the wavelengths at which Townes was working there was no need for the clever solution of a partially reflective surface. Townes simply made a small hole in the resonator through which some of the coherent microwave energy could escape.

Who Invented the Laser?

In one of the longest, most contentious legal battles in the history of the U.S. Patent Office, the American Gordon Gould (1920–) proved that he invented the laser, and he has the patents to prove it.

A *patent* is a form of property, the ownership of which is granted by a government. Patents are granted to inventors for the machines, manufacturing processes, chemicals, genetically engineered plants or animals, or other new and useful inventions that they have created. Significant improvements to existing machines, manufacturing processes, and so on,

American Gordon Gould (1920–   ), the inventor of the laser [Bettman/CORBIS]

may also be patentable. The patent is a statement by the government that the inventor owns the invention in question. Because the owner of the patent is the owner of the invention, he or she is entitled to either prevent others from using or manufacturing the invention in question or to grant others the privilege of using or manufacturing the invention, usually for a fee. The patent is granted for a limited time. Patents make it possible for inventors to profit from their inventions, and without patents there would be less incentive for inventors to invent.

Today, the news media contain many stories about "intellectual property," of which the patent is but one type, but governments have long recognized the importance of patents in promoting inventions. Patents were issued in Italy during the Renaissance, and the concept of patents is part of the U.S. Constitution: Article I, Section 8 states, in part, that the Congress shall have power "To promote the progress of science and useful arts by securing for limited times to authors and inventors the exclusive rights to their respective writings and discoveries."

The laser is one of the most significant inventions of the 20th century. The creation of the laser was an important scientific breakthrough. Nobel Prizes have been awarded for work on or with lasers, and lasers have been used in numerous scientific, medical, and consumer apparatus, where they play an indispensable role. With so much depending on the laser, it was important to determine its rightful inventor, and because the laser is so important, it is not surprising that more than one individual has claimed to have invented it.

To understand the source of confusion, it helps to know about two important aspects of U.S. patent law. First, the patent for an invention is awarded to the first person to invent an object or process and not necessarily the first person to file a patent application. Second, to obtain a patent one need not build a working model for a device; one need only describe the device in sufficient detail so that a person "skilled in the art"—an old-fashioned way of describing someone expert in the relevant specialty—could construct the device from the description. This is why Theodore Maiman is credited with building the first working laser but not with inventing the laser. Gordon Gould fulfilled both requirements for the patent, but as a novice inventor he was a little unclear about the need to produce a working invention.

Gordon Gould graduated from Union College in Schenectady, New York, in 1941. He received a master's degree from Yale University and was working on his Ph.D., which involved using light to raise the energy levels of thallium atoms, a technique that is often referred to as "optical pumping," at Columbia University in 1957, when the idea of the laser occurred to him. (During World War II, he had also worked on the Manhattan Project, the code name for the project that resulted in the creation of atomic weapons.) At the time Gould attended, Columbia University had one of the most successful physics programs in the world. There were many outstanding scientists on the faculty, and many of its graduates later made important discoveries. Among the faculty members was Charles Townes, the inventor of the maser.

Gould was lying in bed on a Saturday night when the idea of a laser occurred to him. Apparently, the idea occurred to him in a flash. But it was more than an idea. As none of his contemporaries did, Gould understood the value of the laser as a tool; he understood its applications. That night Gould got out of bed and began keeping a laboratory notebook in which he carefully described his ideas and sketched diagrams. The title he gave the notebook was "Some rough calculations on the feasibility of LASER: Light Amplification by Stimulated Emission of Radiation." (Recall that the term *laser* was also invented by Gould.)

Gould described a tube containing vapor. A light source would create a population inversion among the atoms contained within the tube. At each end of the tube, there would be mirrors, one of which would be partially transparent, that would cause the photons, produced by stimulated emission, to reflect back and forth, creating an intense and coherent wave. Because the beam could travel large distances while remaining focused, he recognized that it had applications to communications, and because it could be focused into a small volume (and because the energy is inversely proportional to the wavelength), laser light could be used to heat solids and liquids to extremely high temperatures almost instantly.

This was the beginning of Gould's great insights into lasers, and when he had completed nine pages of the notebook, he had each page notarized.

When Gould eventually filed for a patent 18 months later, his application included the use of mirrors to create the oscillations, two methods of creating a population inversion—one used light and the second used "collisions of the second kind," a now-common method that involves collisions between atoms or molecules of various types, a device called a *Q-switch*, and other ideas. Further, he described how one might use lasers to initiate chemical reactions, measure distances, heat materials, communicate, and improve radar. There would be many arguments about who invented the laser, but no one could argue that Gould did not more clearly envision its uses than his contemporaries.

The Q-switch, a device described by Gould in his original application, is an innovation that controls the resonance properties of the laser cavity. Initially, it makes the laser cavity less resonant. This prevents a coherent beam of light from forming because the photons are not reflected between the two ends of the cavity. Meanwhile, energy continues to flow into the medium with the result that a very strong population inversion is created. When a very high proportion of the atoms or molecules are in the higher, metastable state, the switch is reversed so that suddenly the laser cavity becomes highly resonant, at which time a coherent wave sweeps through the highly charged laser medium. This results in the emission of a very brief and powerful laser pulse. The cycle is then repeated. Today, the Q-switch is often utilized in laser designs. Gordon Gould saw deeply into the technology of lasers, as well as how they might be utilized.

Unfortunately for Gould, the team of Townes and Arthur Schawlow (1921–99), a prominent scientist at Bell Labs, also claimed to have invented the laser. Their patent was filed first, and they were far more prominent among scientists than Gould. (Townes was especially prominent after receiving the Nobel Prize.) In the competition, therefore, between Townes and Schawlow on the one hand and Gould on the other, there were few in the scientific establishment willing to consider the possibility that the otherwise obscure Gordon Gould had, in fact, created the laser. As his claim slowly made its way through the legal process, Townes and Schawlow continued to collect licensing fees. (It was later shown that the design that they described in their patent application would not have worked and that one important aspect of their design was identical with an idea that Gould communicated to Townes prior to either one filing a patent application.) Further, as

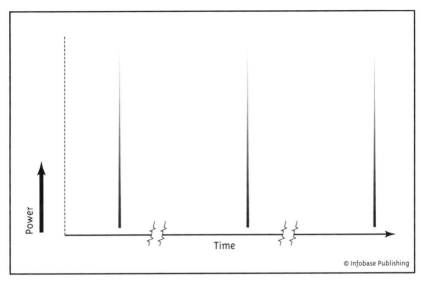

Power curve obtained through the use of a Q-switch. The Q-switch prevents a beam from forming by inhibiting resonance. Instead, a powerful population inversion forms as energy is added to the lasing medium. Once the resonant properties of the lasing medium are restored, a powerful pulse is emitted.

lasers became more commonly used, Gould's claim, were he successful, would have required large payments to him on the part of laser companies and other companies that used lasers. Many companies, including a consortium of laser companies, General Motors, which was already using laser technology, and Bell Laboratories, the most successful research and development laboratory of the 20th century, sought to quash his patent application. They spoke dismissively of him; they even insulted him. One patent attorney for Bell Labs even described Gordon Gould as "a kook." Gould did not invent the laser, asserted the attorney, and " . . . we [Bell Labs] have the patents to prove it." (Bell Labs held some laser patents for inventions that Gould asserted were his own.)

Gould persisted. His claims were examined and reexamined by the Patent and Trademark Office and numerous courts of law. These patents are some of the most carefully scrutinized patents in U.S. history, and 30 years after he first sat upright in bed on a Saturday night and went into the kitchen to get a laboratory notebook, Gordon Gould won his case. He proved in court that he invented the laser, and today, *he* has the patents to prove it.

A Great Variety of Lasers

What was once considered impossible, the creation of a coherent beam of light, turned out to be surprisingly easy. Once Maiman demonstrated that a laser could, indeed, be made to shine, scientists and engineers around the world began creating an extraordinary array of lasers. They discovered that many different materials could be induced to emit laser light and that laser light—or more generally, coherent electromagnetic radiation—could be created at many different wavelengths. The techniques and science involved in the creation of lasers have become so common and widespread that there are now even a number of hobbyists who build their own lasers, and once scientists became more attuned to the existence of the laser phenomenon, they discovered that laser light even occurs naturally. Sunlight creates a population inversion in the upper atmosphere of Mars, for example, where laser light glows without human intervention of any kind.

Initially, much of the motivation for the creation of different types of lasers was purely technical. Scientists and engineers were simply experimenting to see what was possible. They searched for and found a wide variety of materials that could, with the right techniques, be induced to emit laser light. Various gases, liquids, crystalline solids, dyes, and even *plasmas*—gaslike mediums that are composed of collections of charged particles—were all made to lase, or emit, laser light. A number of clever designs were developed for resonators, and the design problems that Maiman originally overcame in the creation of the first laser were quickly solved and resolved by his successors who produced a remarkable array of lasers with widely different properties.

Engineers became more aware of the value of lasers as tools and more attuned to the shortcomings of already created laser designs. As a result, they began to attempt to design lasers with certain predetermined properties. In this endeavor, they have been extremely successful. There are now so many different types of lasers that it is impossible to describe them all here. It is, however, important to develop an appreciation for a few fundamental characteristics of lasers and to understand why these properties are important in matching the right laser to the right task.

Lasers are generally divided into two classes. One class of lasers emits light in a continuous, uninterrupted beam. These are called *continuous wave* (CW) lasers. The second type of laser emits light in short, sharp pulses. These are called pulsed lasers. Maiman's ruby laser, for example, is a pulsed laser. The distinction is important in terms of the ˙

This laser, developed at the Lawrence Livermore National Laboratory for the U.S. Army, is designed to protect against incoming artillery shells, missiles, and other projectiles. [Photo courtesy of Lawrence Livermore National Laboratory]

performance and the design of the laser, and both types of lasers are important.

One can work with a laser only when it is emitting light, of course, and sometimes one wants the laser to emit a steady beam of light. CW lasers have been used to control other lasers and have also proved useful in many industrial and medical applications, but CW lasers are ill-suited for many other applications, and at certain wavelengths it is currently impossible to build a laser that emits a continuous beam. (The first CW laser used carbon dioxide (CO_2) gas as a lasing medium, and the first working CO_2 laser was constructed soon after Maiman's initial success. The details of CO_2 laser design are described in some detail in chapter 6.)

One reason for building a pulsed laser is a technical limitation involving the production of heat: Many pulsed lasers would melt if one tried to operate them continuously. The most extreme example of the phenomenon of heat production occurs in the operation of X-ray lasers. An X-ray laser uses plasma as the lasing medium. Plasma is often described as a fourth form of matter—gases, liquids, and solids are the other three—and does not form easily on Earth. The first task, then, in firing an X-ray laser is to create plasma by stripping electrons away from the atoms with which they were associated to form the gaslike substance composed of electrically charged particles. Next, the ions are raised to a higher energy state to create a population inversion. As they make the transition back to their initial lower state, stimulated emission occurs. This process of creating the plasma and the subsequent population inversion takes tremendous amounts of energy, and the first X-ray lasers were by-products of nuclear explosions. A good deal of research has been done to create more user-friendly X-ray lasers. There is currently a large X-ray laser at the Lawrence Livermore Laboratory in California that emits a pulse with a duration of approximately one billionth of a second, also called a nanosecond. As of this writing, the laser can only emit this extremely brief pulse a maximum of six times a day. The time between pulses is used to cool off the equipment. A little arithmetic shows that the laser must be off more than 10 trillion times longer than it is on in order to prevent the hardware from melting.

Lawrence Livermore also has a second, smaller X-ray laser that can be fired every three to four minutes. It emits two pulses in rapid succession; the longer pulse lasts about a nanosecond, and the other pulse lasts only one trillionth of a second, which is one thousand times briefer than the nanosecond pulse. The time between firings is used to cool the equipment.

Aside from the problem of keeping the equipment cool enough to prevent its destruction, there are also practical reasons why one would want to make a pulsed laser. Scientists, for example, are interested in obtaining information about how chemical bonds are made and broken. (Chemical bonds are the forces that bind atoms into molecules, and chemical reactions involve the making and breaking of chemical bonds as new molecules, called products, are formed from preexisting molecules, called reactants.) Bonds form and dissolve almost instantaneously. The natural timescale for observing these phenomena is determined by the frequency of the molecular vibrations that all molecules undergo. The duration of a single such vibration is measured in a few hundred femtoseconds. (A femtosecond is a quadrillionth of a second. To put it another way: 1,000,000,000,000,000 femtoseconds equals one second.) Lasers can be used to illuminate and examine these processes, but a laser that emitted light for too long a period would smear the data obtained from the experiment in a way that is analogous to the smeared images one obtains when one tries to photograph a fast-moving object, using a camera with a slow shutter speed. To be effective as an investigative tool, the laser must pulse long enough to illuminate the making or breaking of a chemical bond but not so long that it ruins the observation. Lasers now exist that can pulse for less than a tenth of a trillionth of a second or 100 femtoseconds. Pulsed lasers have, for example, also found important uses in the transmission of information, for example. (See chapter 7.)

Another fundamental property of lasers is the wavelength of the electromagnetic waves that each laser emits. (Although the term *laser* was created to distinguish devices that emitted light from the already created maser, which emitted microwave radiation, today the word *laser* is used more broadly to refer to any device that emits coherent electromagnetic radiation.) Recall that all other things being equal, the energy of a laser beam is inversely proportional to its wavelength. This means that the shorter the wavelength of a laser beam, the higher its energy. In particular, if the wavelength is reduced by half, the energy of the beam is doubled. It might seem that for cutting applications, at least, the shorter the wavelength the better it will work, but the situation is more complicated than it might first appear. (One can also increase a beam's energy by increasing the *amplitude* of the light wave, but this will not be discussed here.)

Choosing the right wavelength for a particular application can be complicated because the wavelength of laser light affects more than the energy imparted by the beam. Consider, for example, the problem of

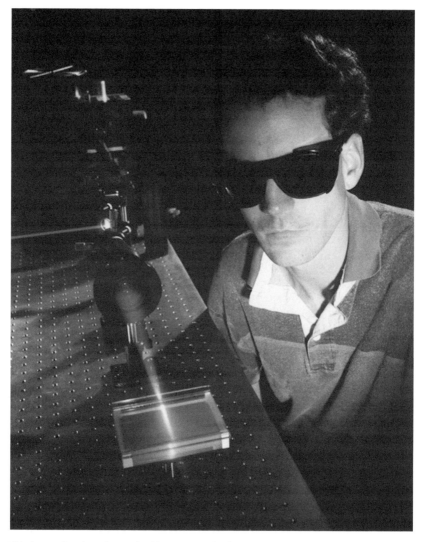

This laser, developed at Oak Ridge National Laboratory, is designed to pass harmlessly through the skin and to penetrate deeply into tissue. [Department of Energy]

cutting with lasers. It is true that lasers are used to cut everything from human flesh to diamonds. In this regard, they are extremely useful, but during the cutting process, they interact with matter in ways that are complicated, not necessarily obvious, and that crucially depend upon the wavelength. For example, focusing a laser that emits a beam with a very short wavelength on flesh may cut flesh by dissolving the covalent bonds that bind the atoms into the long proteins of which humans are composed. If this happens in an uncontrolled way, the result may be injurious to the patient, because the resulting molecular fragments may include some that react to produce other unwanted chemical reactions. On the other hand, a laser that emits electromagnetic waves with very long wavelengths will generally be unable to cut anything. All lasers used in surgery lie in the middle of the electromagnetic spectrum; their wavelengths are longer than microwaves and shorter than X-ray wavelengths.

Creating the right laser for a particular application involves choosing between CW lasers and pulsed lasers (and if the laser is pulsed, creating the optimum pulse characteristics); it involves choosing the right wavelength, and it involves choosing the *power* output that will yield the best results. There are, of course, other design considerations that have not been described here—aiming and controlling the laser, for example—and these aspects of laser design, although they are less central to the subject of this book, are no less essential to the functioning of the final product. Research into new lasers and new laser applications remains a very active area of scientific inquiry.

5

LASERS AND MEDICINE

The first serious applications for lasers were developed in the area of medicine. Ophthalmologists were curious about the effects of lasers on the human eye. They believed that a laser could damage the retina in the same way that looking at the Sun can damage one's retina. In 1960, soon after the first lasers were constructed, a group of ophthalmologists approached Gerard Grosof, a scientist at the research firm TRG, the company employing Gordon Gould, the inventor of the laser, to help them obtain a laser with which to experiment. Grosof in turn approached Gould, and together they removed a ruby laser from TRG's laboratory in the middle of the night—removing the laser was against company policy—and brought it to New York's Bellevue

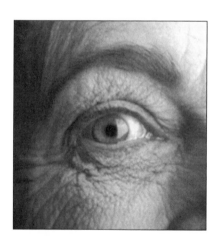

Eye surgery was the first medical application of laser technology. [National Eye Institute, National Institutes of Health]

Hospital, where ophthalmologists planned to test the laser on a rabbit. It was hardly a sophisticated experiment. Despite their concerns about the dangers that lasers posed to the eye, no one wore eye protection. Instead, they aimed the laser at the eye of a rabbit, counted down to zero, closed their eyes, and fired. The doctor holding the rabbit was nervous enough to accidentally smother the rabbit during the experiment by grasping it too firmly. Nevertheless, upon examination of the rabbit's retina, they made a startling discovery: The laser had burned a small hole in the retina of the rabbit but left the intervening material—the cornea, lens, and vitreous humor—unaltered. Today, this may be unremarkable, but at the time, it was a revelation. They had found a way of operating on the retina without disrupting any of the intervening tissue. A few months later, doctors at Columbia-Presbyterian Hospital, also in New York, used a laser to destroy a tumor growing on a human retina.

Matching the Laser to the Medical Application

Blasting away with eyes shut tight while forming a hole in the retina of a rabbit, as the first doctors to test the medical effects of lasers did, is one way to become familiar with the potential of lasers as a surgical tool, but it does not by itself provide sufficient information to enable one to choose the right laser for a particular surgical application. There are now many kinds of lasers operating at many *power* levels, *wavelengths*, and pulse lengths. What are some of the fundamental properties that engineers must take into account in designing a laser for use as a surgical implement?

The first property to take into account is the absorptive property of the tissue under consideration. When light—or any form of electromagnetic radiation—strikes tissue, it may be reflected, absorbed, transmitted, or scattered. A reflected beam does not affect the tissue and so has no effect. If light is not reflected, then it enters the tissue. It may pass directly through (transmission) as ordinary light is transmitted by glass; it may spread out just as sunlight is scattered by fog; or it may be absorbed. Choosing the right laser for a particular application involves controlling these possible outcomes. In the first use of laser light to remove a retinal tumor, for example, the laser beam was transmitted by the tissue that was positioned in front of the retina and absorbed only

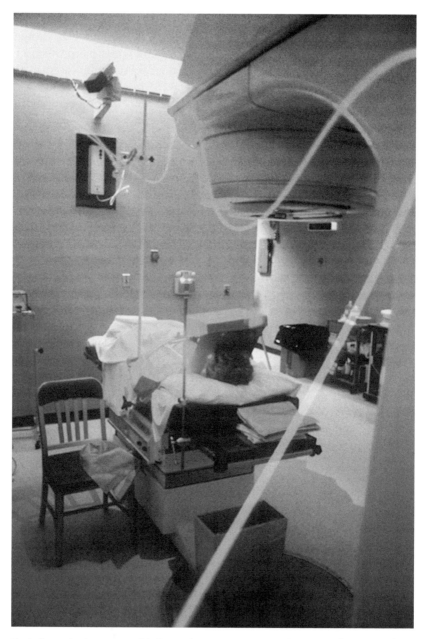

Photodynamic therapy. In this form of cancer treatment, the patient (not shown) is given a cancer-killing drug that becomes active when exposed to light. The laser is designed to emit light that is transmitted through the skin in order to activate the drug. (John Crawford/National Cancer Institute)

by the retina, which explains why the retina was burned but the cornea through which it passed remained unscathed. The first step, therefore, in choosing the right laser involves knowing the physical properties of the tissue that is to be irradiated.

One needs to know which molecules are present in the tissue and which wavelengths those molecules will absorb as well as which wavelengths they will transmit. Carbon dioxide (CO_2) lasers, for example, emit radiation in the infrared portion of the spectrum. Invisible to the naked eye, infrared radiation is absorbed by water molecules. A surgeon who plans to "cut" tissue with high water content—muscle tissue, for example—would do well to consider the use of a CO_2 laser. When used on tissue with high water content, the CO_2 laser vaporizes the water molecules and in the process (provided it is carefully controlled) produces a sharp localized incision. By contrast, bone has a much lower concentration of water, and a CO_2 laser applied to bone is more likely to damage the bone by producing a nonlocalized burn rather than a precise cut. (Even flames are not out of the question.) By choosing a laser that is absorbed by the target molecules and not absorbed by the molecules of neighboring tissues, it is possible to restrict one's cuts to the tissue of interest.

Having identified the physical properties of the tissues of interest, the next step in choosing the right laser is choosing a suitable wavelength. The shorter the wavelength—all other things being equal—the higher the energy of the beam. The effects of a laser on a particular tissue depend on the wavelength in two other, more fundamental ways.

First, the depth to which a laser beam will penetrate is a function of its wavelength. Scientists use the concept of "extinction length" to describe this phenomenon. The extinction length of a particular laser on a given tissue is the depth of tissue required to absorb 90 percent of the laser's energy. For example, CO_2 lasers emit *electromagnetic waves* that are relatively long (in the infrared), and this results in a shallow penetration depth. A short pulse from a CO_2 laser aimed at the skin will be absorbed by the skin. It will not penetrate deep into the tissues beneath the skin. (A longer pulse of energy at these wavelengths can go deeper because the heat generated at the skin will be transmitted to the tissues below by the process of conduction.) By contrast, a neodymium:yttrium aluminum garnet laser (abbreviated Nd:YAG) emits electromagnetic waves with a wavelength of 1,064 nanometers, and a short pulse of radiation at this wavelength will penetrate to a depth of a few millimeters. Therefore, choosing the right wavelength involves knowing how deeply into the tissue one wants to penetrate.

The second factor to consider is the way the laser cuts. Shorter wavelengths can break the covalent bonds that hold molecules together, whereas longer wavelengths may cause a phase change—for example, liquid water may vaporize—in the tissue that is irradiated. The way that the laser cuts determines the type of damage that it does, an important consideration when the operation is over and the time has come to heal.

Finally, the manner in which the laser is applied is critical. Designers need to pay extra attention to the way in which tissue is heated. Lasers are used to deliver radiant energy, that is, the electromagnetic energy that emanates from the laser will, upon absorption by the target molecules, be changed into molecular vibrations, which is just another way of saying heat. The absorption of electromagnetic energy happens virtually instantaneously. But once the heated molecules begin to vibrate they will transfer their vibrations to other nearby molecules, which, in turn, transfer some of that vibration to other molecules still farther away. Think of the molecules of which tissue is composed as tiny spheres, each sphere connected to its neighbors by a collection of springs. If one sphere is shaken violently and continuously, the vibrations will eventually be transmitted to many spheres, and soon the whole mass will be vibrating. This is, roughly speaking, the way that heat travels via the process of conduction. It is, in comparison to the transfer of radiant energy, a slow process. Conduction is a phenomenon that designers generally want to minimize.

The danger associated with conduction is that all molecules in the region, not just the target molecules, become heated. The result is that all the molecules in the region are damaged by the heat resulting from contact with the laser, because the laser produced a generalized burn rather than a precise cut. For this reason, engineers prefer to use higher-power lasers. A low-power laser requires the surgeon to concentrate the beam on the target for extended periods of time. During that time much of the energy of the laser diffuses into the surrounding tissue due to the process of conduction. By contrast, if a high-power laser beam (of the right wavelength) is applied, the energy is absorbed quickly—quickly relative to the much slower process of conduction— with the result that the target tissue vaporizes almost instantaneously. If the laser is then shut off so that no additional energy is transferred into the tissue, there will be relatively little conduction because the total amount of energy transferred was not great. What was large was the *rate* at which the energy was transferred. The result is that while the target tissue is vaporized, the surrounding tissue is unaffected.

These pulsed lasers may have a duty cycle—the ratio of time-on to time-off—of about 1:2 or 1:3, but under certain conditions the laser may be off many times longer than it is on. It depends on the application and the specific properties of the laser.

Engineers have also created lasers that emit light in the violet and ultraviolet parts of the spectrum for use in surgery. These transfer energy into the tissue so quickly that shock waves are produced that tear the target tissues. When this is done in a controlled way, there is virtually no change in the temperature of the surrounding tissue. These are sometimes called "cold" lasers, because they are so effective at cutting tissue without causing temperature change. To return to the sphere and spring analogy used earlier, this is analogous to grabbing a single sphere and shaking it just once, but with sufficient force, so that all the attached springs snap off. One can imagine that if this were done quickly enough there would be little vibration transferred to the neighboring spheres.

No matter the details, the goal is always the same: Heat the target molecules so that they vaporize, and do it so quickly that heat is not transferred to neighboring tissues by the process of conduction.

Cutting Flesh

To be sure, a laser is a more technologically sophisticated tool than a scalpel, but this alone is not sufficient reason to warrant its use in the operating room. In order to justify their greater expense and potential hazards, lasers must demonstrate marked advantages over scalpels and other more traditional surgical implements.

One advantage lasers have over other surgical implements is their potential for precision. Lasers can be constructed to emit beams much thinner than a human hair. Such lasers enable the surgeon to make narrower cuts and so do less damage in the process. These narrow-beam lasers make it possible to vaporize only those cells necessary to accomplish a given aim, while leaving the surrounding tissue intact, and because less damage is done, the healing process may be accelerated. But not every laser designed for medical use emits a narrow beam. Some lasers are designed to emit beams a few millimeters wide. The width of the beam depends upon the application. A wider beam might be used to vaporize regions of skin in the treatment of malignancies or certain skin pigmentation conditions. In these situations, the laser beam is "swept" across the skin, destroying large areas of cells close to the surface. The resulting damaged, sometimes charred, tissue is removed by gentle scrubbing, and then the procedure is repeated as necessary. These lasers can be designed and operated so that the depth of the affected tissue can be carefully controlled and no more tissue is destroyed than is intended.

Lasers can also produce an effect called *photocoagulation*. When small blood vessels are cut with a laser, the beam of the laser may simultaneously seal the blood vessels. The result is that bleeding is minimized. Sometimes this is a side benefit: Chosen for their cutting precision, these lasers also reduce bleeding around the wound. But some doctors, for example those specializing in gastroenterology—that branch of medicine concerned with the stomach and intestines—have made use of this effect in the treatment of bleeding ulcers. Their goal is to stanch the bleeding of patients in a way that is as least invasive as possible. The laser is one tool that has been used to accomplish this goal successfully. The preferred laser, generally a Nd:YAG, is delivered to the ulcer along a very fine fiber-optic cable and then focused on the area in question. Energy is emitted in pulses of approximately one-half second duration. Coagulation occurs; the bleeding stops; the operation is a success. Despite the value of the technique, there are other non-laser techniques—heater probes, for example—that have proven just as successful and are far less expensive—proof that the laser, though valuable, is no panacea.

Lasers have also been used to stop bleeding of the retina. In this application, they have no equal, because as previously mentioned, certain wavelengths of laser light can deliver energy to the back of the eye without damaging the intervening tissue.

In addition to their advantages, lasers introduce new and sometimes unexpected hazards. The most obvious hazard is to the vision of the patient and medical personnel. No matter how powerful the light emanating from a laser, the cornea and lens of the eye focus the light even more sharply on the retina, where the light-sensitive structures called cones and rods are located. Under normal lighting conditions, medical personnel will be using that part of the eye called the fovea centralis, a small region on the retina where most of the cones, the cells used for day vision, reside. A small burn on this small region can cause a severe and permanent loss of vision. Of course, everyone on the staff knows not to look into a laser beam. The most frequent cause of accidental exposure is the unintended reflection of the laser beam off a reflective surface, usually the metallic instruments used during surgery. Eye protection is essential.

A less obvious hazard occurs because of the way that lasers affect tissue. Lasers employed in the cutting of tissue—but not those used in photocoagulation—are designed to generate sufficient heat to char or vaporize tissue almost instantaneously. When these lasers are working properly, they are generating airborne, possibly hazardous, substances. Studies have shown that spores and viruses can survive the vaporization of the tissues in which they are located and become airborne. This, of course, is a cause of concern. (Notice that this issue does not arise when one uses more traditional cutting implements.) As a consequence, patients and staff must have good respiratory protection, and the area around the laser as well as the room as a whole must be well ventilated.

Despite these difficulties, lasers have an enormous number of uses in the operating room. One interesting application that shows the unique nature of lasers as a medical tool occurs when they are used to remove kidney stones. Urine contains minerals that are suspended in solution. If, however, the concentration of such minerals becomes too great, they begin to precipitate out of solution and form small concretions within the kidneys. These concretions further combine with organic matter, and the result is a kidney stone. The larger the stone, the more surface area there is for additional accretion, and the larger it becomes. Large stones can interfere with the working of the kidney and should be removed. There are a variety of ways of dealing with kidney stones, but one method is to use a pulsed laser with a wavelength of 504 nanometers. (Light at this wavelength is green.) The light is delivered via a fiber optic cable. High-energy pulses are concentrated on the kidney stone, which cause part of it to vaporize. The process is so quick and violent that a shock wave is produced that causes the rest of the stone to fragment. A clever benefit of using green light is that it is not well absorbed by hemoglobin, an important constituent of blood. Therefore, if the beam misses the kidney stone and strikes other tissue in the kidney, the damage is minimized because most of the energy is not absorbed.

Eye Surgery

As described at the beginning of this chapter, eye surgery is one of the oldest and most familiar applications of laser technology, and as laser technology continues to improve, the results of laser eye surgery become increasingly predictable. The most fundamental improvements

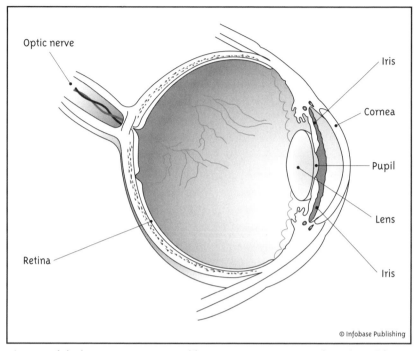

Optic nerve

Iris

Cornea

Pupil

Lens

Retina

Iris

© Infobase Publishing

Diagram of the human eye. Lasers enable surgeons to operate on the retina without damaging the intervening tissue.

are found in the areas of laser control and a better understanding of the physics involved. One of the most common medical applications of the laser occurs in the area of vision correction.

With respect to vision correction, the problem laser surgery seeks to address is called refractive error. To appreciate how ophthalmologists seek to correct refractive error through the use of lasers, it is important to appreciate precisely what refractive error is and how it arises. A mechanical, very unromantic, way of describing the eye is as a device for converting electromagnetic energy from the visible part of the electromagnetic spectrum into electrical signals. The electrical signals are conveyed to the brain via the optic nerve, and the brain interprets the signals received. Essentially, eyes are for looking, and brains are for seeing.

At the front of the eye is the cornea. It covers and protects the front of the eye and also helps focus the light that enters the eye. Behind the cornea is the opening that permits light to enter the eye. That opening is called the pupil. The pupil is small and circular. It looks black, but it is not. The pupil seems dark for the same reason that windows on a house appear dark on a sunny day. The windows are transparent, but the rooms behind them are darker than the outside environment. Similarly, the pupil is the window of the eye. It appears dark because the interior of the eye, which is transparent, is darker than the outside. Surrounding the pupil is the iris, the colored part of the eye. The iris regulates the amount of light entering the eye by opening and closing. Behind the pupil is the lens, which further focuses the incoming light so that a sharp image appears on the retina. The shape of the lens can be changed somewhat as the ligaments around it are tightened or relaxed. This enables one to bring a slightly blurred object into focus. There are, however, limitations to what the lens can do, and despite its name, much of the work in focusing the incoming light is done by the cornea rather than the lens. (The interior of the eye is filled with a transparent material, made mostly of water, called the vitreous humor.)

When the image that is formed on the retina is not clear, the brain is unable to form a clear picture from the electrical images that it receives. The most common reason for a blurry image on the retina involves difficulty focusing the image properly. Ophthalmologists have long known that (in theory) one way to correct blurred vision is to operate directly on the cornea with the aim of changing its shape. Changing the shape of the cornea changes where and how the light entering the eye comes to a focus. Early efforts at sculpting the cornea were done mechanically, and they were very crude. The first attempts, developed in the late 1940s and early 1950s, involved slicing a disc-shaped piece of cornea off the front of the eye, freezing it, grinding the frozen tissue into the appropriate shape on a special-purpose lathe, and then replacing it. The technique was crude, and it was used only in the most extreme cases.

Today, the same concepts involved in cornea sculpting are carried out with lasers. The procedure begins by using a blade called a microkeratome to open a thin flap on the front of the cornea. The flap is opened much like the hood of a car, exposing the tissue underneath. Next, a high-energy, pulsed laser, operating in the ultraviolet portion of the spectrum, begins to cut the cornea. The duration of the pulses are in the nanosecond—one billionth of a second—range. These brief, high-energy pulses enable the user to destroy selected tissue segments without damaging neighboring tissues by thermal conduction. Layers of tissue on the order of a micrometer (one millionth of a meter) are removed with each pulse of the laser. With such small tolerances, it would not be correct to say that the doctor is performing the operation. Such levels of precision are far beyond what any individual could achieve. The laser is computer controlled. The machine follows its program, directing and firing the laser,

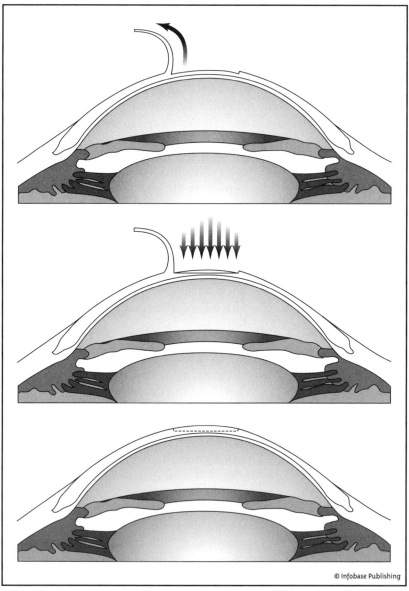

© Infobase Publishing

Using a laser to correct refractive error. First a flap is opened to expose the tissue underneath. Next, tiny sections of the cornea are removed. When the desired shape is achieved, the flap is closed.

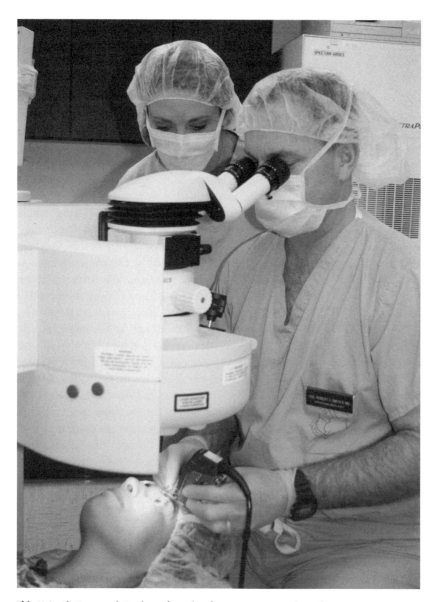

This U.S. Air Force aviator is undergoing laser eye surgery in order to correct refractive error. (U.S. Air Force Photo by Sue Campbell)

which continues to ablate, or remove, portions of tissue until it has pared the cornea down to some predetermined shape. The flap is then closed—no stitches are necessary—and provided all goes well, the incision soon heals, and the patient's vision is improved.

Tattoo Removal

The process of tattooing involves introducing pigment underneath the skin. Beneath the skin the pigment accumulates in the form of granules. The color of the granules depends on their chemical composition. The metals mercury and chromium, for example, are often used to make red- and green-colored pigments, respectively. The pigment particles measure about 150 to 180 micrometers in diameter. As a general rule, tattoos are easier to create than remove. Various techniques exist for removing tattoos; they involve using chemicals, mechanical abrasion, or lasers.

Tattoos are usually described as permanent, but the design generally fades slowly with time. The fading process takes many years, during which time the body's own immune system slowly attacks the granules of pigment, with the result that colors fade and the edges of the design become less sharp. This process can be greatly accelerated by the use of lasers.

Ruby lasers are often used in tattoo removal. As mentioned in chapter 3, ruby lasers emit light at a wavelength of 694.3 nanometers. Many of the dyes used in tattoos absorb energy at this wavelength more readily than does skin. Consequently, if the light from a ruby laser is concentrated on a tattoo, the pigments of which the tattoo is composed become hotter faster than the surrounding tissue. The difference will not matter if a low-power laser is used, because then the pigments will heat slowly and the heat will have sufficient time to diffuse (by conduction) from the pigment granules to the surrounding tissue. But if the energy is transferred quickly, one can obtain a large temperature difference between the granules and skin in which they are embedded. It is this brief pulse of energy that is the key to laser techniques for removing tattoos.

The laser first releases a short powerful burst—generally

Tattoo enthusiast, 1907. Until the development of laser-based tattoo removal techniques, the process of removing tattoos was difficult, slow, painful, inefficient, and often involved some scarring. (Library of Congress, Prints and Photographs Division)

obtained via *Q-switching*—for about 30 nanoseconds. The pigment becomes much hotter than the surrounding tissue almost instantly. Shock waves are generated that pulverize the pigment granules. In fact, the skin appears white for 15 to 20 minutes following tattoo-removal treatment with a laser because of steam that is generated underneath the skin by sudden heating and resulting shock waves. The shattered granules that result are more easily destroyed by the immune system. It takes several weeks to determine the success of the treatment.

One laser treatment may not be sufficient, and there is a waiting period between visits to give the body a chance to remove the tiny particles that are the result of the process. The way that the tattoo responds to the laser depends on the colors that were used in its creation. Some pigments absorb the light better than others. The more efficiently the pigment absorbs light at a wavelength of 694.3 nanometers, the more effective the treatment will be. The density of the pigment within the skin also affects the outcome of each treatment. There are no guarantees, but laser treatments represent one of the best ways of removing tattoos. The least traumatic, least expensive way of being tattoo-free, however, remains forgoing the tattooing experience entirely.

6

LASERS IN INDUSTRY

This researcher oversees a process that uses a laser cutter to fabricate fuel cells. [Pacific Northwest National Laboratory]

By 1962, only two years after the creation of the first *laser*, engineers had begun to apply lasers to the problems of cutting, drilling, and welding materials. One early, oft-repeated experiment involved drilling holes in razor blades with a laser, and for a while the power of a laser was informally measured in "gillettes," the number of razor blades through which a laser beam could burn.

In contrast to what is shown in science fiction films, where drilling, cutting, and welding with lasers is simply a matter of pointing the device and pulling the switch, actual industrial applications are complex procedures. Many people assume that it is a relatively simple matter of substituting a laser beam for a drill bit, a laser beam for a pair of scissors, or a laser beam for a welding torch. However, when lasers are introduced into an industrial environment, they create problems of their own—problems that are unique to the use of light as a drilling, cutting, or welding tool. (When a laser is used to cut steel, for example, it produces a gas consisting of vaporized steel. Designers must take into account how much vapor is produced and what becomes of it.)

There is also the difference between theory and practice: Industrial processes introduce demands on their lasers that are different from those experienced by researchers in the laboratory. In the laboratory, a laser must perform a task only several times a day. At night, the researchers go home and the laser remains idle. In a manufacturing environment, however, a laser may be called upon to perform the same task many thousands of times, day and night, for weeks or even months at a time. No matter how well a device works in the laboratory, if it is not extremely robust, it has no place on the factory floor. Finally, as with any tool, lasers are subject to cost-benefit analysis. Lasers are often more expensive than more traditional tools, so before a company purchases a laser, it must be convinced that the quality and quantity of work performed by the laser justifies its higher cost. Sometimes lasers have met these criteria; sometimes they have not.

Matching the Laser to the Industrial Application

As a general rule, lasers have several advantages over more traditional cutting, drilling, and welding tools. Some of these advantages should sound familiar. They are the same characteristics that make lasers valuable as surgical tools. One of the advantages shared by medical and industrial lasers involves the precision with which they can be programmed to operate. Another advantage is that lasers can transfer energy to the target very quickly and in the process melt or vaporize a very small region without affecting material outside the target area. Finally, lasers work at the speed of light. Consequently, they can perform their tasks quickly, and this can lead to gains in manufacturing efficiency.

To see how these very broad considerations are implemented in practice, consider two of the most common industrial lasers, the CO_2 and the Nd:YAG lasers. These lasers were mentioned in chapter 5 in terms

Notice that the wings of this modified F-16 aircraft are not mirror images of each other. The left wing has been outfitted with a titanium sleeve containing millions of tiny laser-drilled holes. A low-pressure area is created inside the sleeve that causes air to flow down through the holes into the wing, and this reduces turbulence along the wing's surface. [NASA]

of their effects on tissue. It is now instructive to see how these lasers produce their light, and the way that their designs affect their value as industrial tools.

The CO_2 laser was one of the first types of lasers constructed, and it remains one of the most popular of all laser types. It consists of a tube filled with a mixture of three types of gas. Helium is the main constituent. There are also approximately equal amounts of nitrogen and carbon dioxide gas. The exact percentages vary from one design to the next, but helium often comprises about 75 percent of the total mixture. This three-gas mixture is the medium in which the light is produced and corresponds functionally to the ruby crystal in Maiman's original laser. An electric current is passed through the gas mixture, which excites the nitrogen molecules to a higher energy level. (The electric current takes the place of the flash lamp in the ruby laser.) The nitrogen molecules transfer their energy to the carbon dioxide molecules via collisions, and it is the energy that is transferred during these collisions that creates the population inversion among the CO_2 molecules. (The CO_2 molecules play essentially the same role in the gas mixture that the chromium atoms played in Maiman's laser.) Just as with the ruby laser, one end of the tube holding the gas mixture is highly reflective, but because the waves produced are not in the visible part of the *spectrum*—CO_2 lasers produce invisible infrared *electromagnetic waves*—the mirror is made of different materials. Sometimes copper-coated glass is used; sometimes the metal molybdenum is used as a mirror, and other materials are used as well. The opposite end of the tube, the end through which the laser shines, cannot be made of glass because with respect to infrared waves, glass is opaque. One material that is sometimes used to create a partially reflective material is zinc selenide. Under certain conditions, sodium chloride (table salt) is sometimes used as well.

The electromagnetic waves produced in the excited gas *oscillate* back and forth in the tube and are amplified via the process of *stimulated emission*. Carbon dioxide lasers are easily made more powerful by lengthening the tube in which they are produced, and compared to many other lasers they are remarkably efficient: A high-power CO_2 laser will convert approximately 20 percent of all the electrical energy that enters the tube into laser energy. This means, however, that 80 percent of the electrical energy that enters the tube must be removed to prevent the equipment from overheating. This is part of the reason that the principal constituent of the mixture is helium. It improves the ability of the gas to conduct heat, and this makes it easier to remove heat from the tube. The laser operates efficiently only if the gas mixture is kept cool.

The Nd:YAG laser is very similar to the ruby laser. It uses a crystal—called the yttrium-aluminum-garnet crystal (hence YAG)—through which neodymium is diffused. (The neodymium plays the same role as the chromium in the ruby laser.) Visible light usually is directed into the crystal by some sort of flash lamp, and it is this light that creates the population inversion. This is the most common method of initiating a population inversion, but increasingly, Nd:YAG lasers are pumped with another laser. Laser excitation of the lasing medium increases the efficiency of the Nd:YAG laser. Because the electromagnetic radiation produced by the Nd:YAG is almost in the visible range—the *wavelength* of the light emitted by this laser is a little longer than that of red light—the beam behaves in a way that is very similar to light waves. In particular, they travel through glass without difficulty, something that the beam emitted by the CO_2 laser cannot do. This proves to be an important advantage.

Carbon dioxide lasers have several advantages over the Nd:YAG lasers. It is a relatively simple matter to make a powerful CO_2 laser:

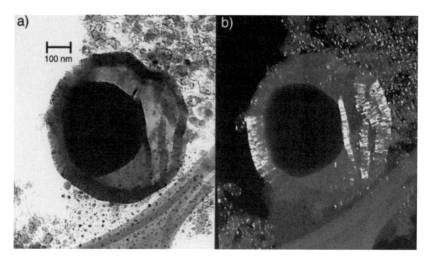

Two images of the same laser-drilled hole. At a few hundred nanometers across, this type of precision work can be accomplished only with a laser. [NASA]

Provide sufficient electrical power to a sufficiently long tube. The longer the tube, the more powerful the laser. Further, CO_2 lasers can be operated in CW (*continuous wave*) mode or pulsed, in part, because they are relatively easy to cool, and they are efficient. True, an efficiency of 20 percent means that 80 percent of the input energy is wasted, but 20 percent is very good for a laser. By contrast, an ordinary, optically pumped Nd:YAG laser may well have an efficiency of less than 1 percent. Much of the energy that enters this laser's crystal is converted to heat and must be removed in order to avoid damaging the crystal. But even with a cooling system, the Nd:YAG crystal is difficult to keep cool because producing the laser beam rapidly generates heat inside the crystal, and heat moves toward the surface, where it can be removed, by conduction. The difference in the rates of heat generation and heat conduction explains why it is easy to overheat the crystal. For this reason, Nd:YAG lasers are always operated in brief pulses. Finally, CO_2 lasers are robust. A well-made tube of gas is hard to break and relatively inexpensive to replace. The crystal that makes up the heart of the Nd:YAG laser is, by contrast, both more fragile and more expensive to replace.

Nd:YAG lasers, however, have their own advantages over the CO_2 variety. The most important is that the wavelength of light emitted by the Nd:YAG laser is easily transmitted along an optical fiber. (Recall that the glass is opaque to the electromagnetic waves emitted by the CO_2 laser, and so light from a CO_2 laser cannot be transmitted along an optical fiber.) Therefore, one can place the Nd:YAG laser in one location and transmit its beam to another location via optical fiber. By contrast, a CO_2 laser beam is generally transmitted directly through the air and redirected—around a corner, for example—by mirrors. This makes transmission of a CO_2 laser beam more susceptible to interruption, and water vapor, which is always present in the air, is a particular problem in this regard because it absorbs some of the laser energy emitted by the CO_2 laser.

The other advantage that Nd:YAG lasers have over their CO_2 counterparts has to do with the way that laser energy at the wavelength of an Nd:YAG laser affects the materials against which it is directed. For example, aluminum reflects more electromagnetic energy at a wavelength of about 10 micrometers (μm), or 10 millionths of a meter, which is the approximate wavelength of light emitted by the CO_2 laser than it does at a wavelength of about one μm, which is the approximate wavelength emitted by the Nd:YAG laser. As a consequence, substantially more power (about 40 percent) is required from the CO_2 laser to cut aluminum than is required from the Nd:YAG laser, because so much of the energy generated by the CO_2 laser is initially reflected away by the aluminum.

These are only some of the considerations that must be taken into account in choosing the right laser for a particular application. The use of electromagnetic radiation as an industrial tool involves a great deal of physics. It is not simply a matter of point and shoot.

Cutting Metal and Drilling Diamonds

To understand both the advantages and disadvantages of using lasers to cut and drill into very hard materials, it is advantageous to examine the accompanying diagram; it illustrates several important properties of a cutting laser. First, the laser is a noncontact instrument. This makes it ideal for cutting material that is fragile or easily damaged, and if the material is very hard, the laser will not dull. It can also cut patterns that are too intricate for a mechanical blade to cut. Next, notice in the illustration that although the light rays emitted by the laser are initially parallel, they are passed through a lens, the purpose of which is to bring those rays to a focus. The location in space at which all the rays converge is called the focal point, and it is here that the best cutting occurs. In

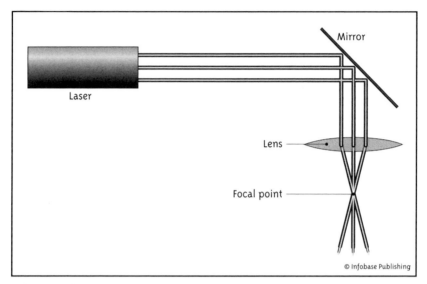

© Infobase Publishing

Schematic of a cutting laser. Notice that the highest intensity of laser energy is achieved at the focal point. The intensity drops off above and below the focal point.

an industrial laser, cutting may occur away from the focal point as well because the laser beam already has a very high energy density, meaning that it delivers a great deal of power per unit area. The beam is often powerful enough that the mirrors used in many cutting lasers must be water cooled. Nevertheless, by bringing all the rays to a focus, one can create an even higher energy density and so cut faster and more precisely than would otherwise be possible.

Now take a closer look at the geometry of the laser beam in the diagram. After passing through the lens, the laser beam takes on the shape of a conic, a geometric object that has the shape of two ice-cream cones joined at their apexes. As described in the previous paragraph, this conical geometry enables the designer to obtain a higher energy density at the focal point for the same amount of laser energy consumption, but it also has the effect of limiting the depth at which the laser cuts. After passing through the focal point, the light cone becomes ever wider, with the result that the energy density far from the focal point is quite low. As the energy density diminishes so does the laser's ability to cut. One can compensate for this effect to some extent by using a lens with a long focal length. (The focal length is the distance from focal point to the lens.) A longer focal length makes the sides of the conic steeper and so keeps the light rays closer together longer. Despite this technique, cutting lasers are usually used on relatively thin materials.

Recall that cutting lasers actually vaporize rather than cut the
target material. In other words,
they cause a *phase* change: The
solid material is turned into a
vapor. Some of this vapor will
condense on the target material,
both on the upper and lower side
of the cut, and make for a slightly
rough edge. Some of the vaporized material also floats in the air
above the cut. Airborne vapor can
absorb energy from the laser, or
reflect it away, before the light
reaches the target. The result is a
degraded laser beam and less effi-

Robot-controlled laser cutter. Laser
cutters can often work at speeds and at
levels of precision that are not possible
with mechanical tools, and, of course,
lasers never become dull. [U.S. Department
of Energy]

cient cutting. One way of minimizing this effect is to blow the vapor
away from the cutting zone, where it can be evacuated by exhaust fans.
Engineers have found, however, that if they use oxygen to blow away
the vapor produced by the laser they can speed the cutting rates by
causing the metal at the focal point to combust in a controlled fashion.
Visually, this makes for some spectacular sparks.

Lasers are also used as drills. Just as for cutting lasers, laser drills
vaporize material rather than drill through it mechanically. Laser drills
are based on essentially the same concepts as laser cutters, and the
diagram used to describe the principles by which lasers cut also applies
to how they can be used to drill. In particular, by using a lens to focus
a laser beam for drilling, one obtains a conical rather than cylindrical
hole. As with laser cutting tools, the conical shape of the resulting hole
can be minimized by using a long focal length lens, but that simply
reduces the effect; it does not eliminate it. And there is another effect
to consider: Some of the vapor produced by the process condenses and
solidifies around the edge of the region that was vaporized. The result
is a crater-shaped hole that, depending on the application, may need
some mechanical finishing. Drilling large holes is more problematic
because using a laser to create a large hole requires a great deal of
energy, and in the process of drilling the hole large amounts of vapor
are produced. The production of the vapor can interfere with further
drilling by absorbing or reflecting the laser energy. For these reasons,
most large holes are still drilled mechanically.

While there are significant limitations to the use of lasers as drills,
and not every drilling task is suitable for a laser, lasers are widely used

in certain applications. One application in which they excel involves drilling very small holes. This is one application that is unsuitable for mechanical drills. Very small bits become dull quickly and break easily. By contrast, lasers, because they are noncontact tools, never become dull or break. (The mirrors and lenses must, however, be protected and kept clean.) Provided that the material is not too thick, therefore, lasers can be used to drill small holes quickly.

One of the classic applications of laser drills involves drilling holes in diamonds. Diamonds, renowned for their hardness, are used in the process of forming wires. Metal is forced through the hole in the diamond to form a wire. The holes are generally quite small, and drilling a small hole through one of the hardest substances in the world with a traditional drill bit is difficult, expensive, and time consuming. This is an ideal application for the laser drill, which vaporizes, rather than cuts, its way through the diamond in a minute rather than in a day. The hole still needs to be smoothed and polished because of the way that the laser created it, but most of the work in drilling diamonds is done by the laser.

Cutting Cloth

The textile business is one of the biggest and most competitive businesses in the world. Everyone needs clothes, and many consumers buy more clothes than they wear. One way of meeting this demand has been to use steel blades to cut thick stacks of material into clothing components, assemble the components into clothes that are as uniform with respect to style and size as possible and then to ship them to stores. The system has its drawback. Most consumers know the frustration of finding an appealing style but being unable to find the right size. Alternatively, the store may stock many unappealing items in just the right size. These situations have long been consequences of textile manufacturing technology just as they were a part of automotive technology for many years. The Ford Model T automobile, for example, was once available only in the color black. When Henry Ford was asked if one could purchase the car in the color of one's choice, Ford responded with the famous line, "You can buy it in any color, as long as it's black."

When lasers were first introduced into the textile business, they were just one more tool in a mass production business. They have certain advantages over mechanical tools, advantages that by now should sound familiar: On some fabrics, they make a smoother cut, and when operated properly, they can cut with far more precision. (Some industrial lasers can be focused with sufficient precision to etch paper.)

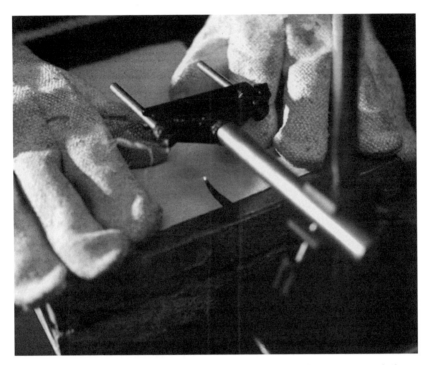

Demonstration of a laser cutting cloth. Coupled with a robot, lasers can cut cloth quickly, accurately, cheaply, and without leaving a fringe along the edge. They have made it possible to create clothing in entirely new ways. (SSPL/The Image Works)

Further, because they are a noncontact tool, they never become dull. But the latest trend in the use of lasers in the textile industry involves the process of mass customization, a revolutionary approach to making clothing and shoes more attractive to the consumer, an approach that would surely have fascinated Henry Ford.

Mass production is a term that has traditionally meant large numbers of identical products. The quality of a particular name brand might be high or it might be low, but the goal of mass production techniques was to ensure uniform quality across production runs—that is, all objects manufactured according to the same plan should be identical not just in style and size but in quality as well. The process results in the production of large amounts of clothing that no one wants to buy. Mass customization is a concept that is becoming increasingly popular in the textile industry. The goal of mass customization is to preserve what is best about mass production—uniformity of quality and relatively low cost—and at the same time to manufacture only clothes that the consumer wants to buy.

Mass customization may seem to be a self-contradictory term, but there are clothing and shoe stores that are already beginning to implement the idea, which works as follows: First, the customer chooses a particular style from an array of pictures or samples. Next, the customer is measured for fit. This step is increasingly done with lasers, which provide measurements more quickly and often more accurately than one can obtain with a tape measure. (See chapter 9 for information about how lasers are used as measurement devices.) Depending on the item to be purchased and the method used in measurement, many thousands of individual measurements may be made on the customer over the course of a minute or two. The measurements are then used as input for a computer program that computes the dimensions of the pattern to be used in the creation of the shoe or garment. These computations include both the sizes of the individual pieces that make up the item as well as the way that the pieces are to be cut from the bulk material. This second factor is important to reduce waste and so increase profit. The information is sent to the factory, where, for example, a single bolt of fabric is unrolled and cut (vaporized) with a computer-controlled laser—an ideal application for a laser because the material is thin and, if the item is to be affordable, the work must be done as quickly and accurately as possible. The individual pieces are then assembled and shipped to the consumer. The result is a pair of shoes or a garment in the material, style, pattern, color, and so on, of the consumer's choice all assembled to fit perfectly. The mass production of unique items is a welcome change from the enormous array of ill-fitting garments and shoes carried by stores the world over. It is a technology that would surely have astonished Henry Ford.

Laser Welding

Welding is another common laser application, but the physics of welding are quite different from the physics of cutting steel and cloth or drilling steel or diamonds. Cutting and drilling generally involve vaporizing small sections of the material in question. By contrast, welding involves melting. The process of welding is in some ways a little more delicate than that of vaporizing: If one applies too much power, the material may vaporize rather than melt; if one applies too little power, the process of conduction causes too much of the energy to dissipate into the surrounding material. In the latter case, either the energy is conducted away from the target before the metal melts and no melting occurs or, if enough energy is supplied, the melted area becomes too large. Identifying and controlling the many factors that affect a successful laser weld is an important and very active discipline in applied science. Progress has been made—lasers are now an important and widely used tool on automotive assembly lines, for example—but there is still much work to accomplish in understanding and better utilizing this process.

The first problem to overcome in making a successful weld involves transferring enough, but not too much, energy to the material. Keep in mind that metals are often fairly reflective, and electromagnetic radiation that is reflected from the target material is wasted in the sense that it has no effect on the target. However, if it is reflected back at the laser, it may damage the laser itself. In order for the laser to affect the metal, its energy must be absorbed. The absorptivity, which is the percentage of the incident radiation absorbed by the target material, of various common metals depends on a variety of factors, including the finish of the material, its temperature, and the wavelength of the laser beam. In most cases, however, absorptivity is surprisingly low. For example, aluminum at room temperature will initially absorb only about 2 percent of the electromagnetic radiation emitted at a wavelength of 10.6 micrometers (μm), the wavelength characteristic of a CO_2 laser, and it will absorb only about 6 percent of incident radiation

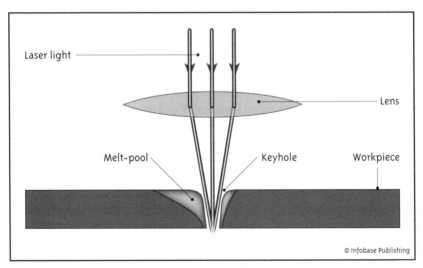

Welding with a laser often involves forming the "keyhole," a narrow V-shaped region of melted metal. As the laser burrows into the metal, vaporized metal is ejected upward.

at a wavelength of 1.06 µm, the wavelength of an Nd:YAG laser, and these are the two most common lasers used in welding. This is one reason that very powerful lasers are used in industrial applications: When the laser beam is first applied to the target, most of the energy has no effect because initially most of the energy is not absorbed.

Once the metal melts, however, the absorptivity of the target metal generally increases dramatically. The absorptivity of a CO_2 laser beam, for example, jumps from a few percent to 60 or even 80 percent. The melted area begins to deepen, and a pool of liquid metal forms. A great many interesting phenomena occur almost simultaneously at this point and often last for only a fraction of a second. For example, if the melted area deepens into a V-shape, called a keyhole, the surface of the liquid curves. This concentrates the laser beam toward the center of the region. The energy that is not initially absorbed by the liquid is not generally reflected away from the metal but is instead reflected to the other side of the keyhole, further increasing the absorption of the laser beam. This all happens so fast that a pool of molten metal is formed inside a V-shaped pocket of relatively cool solid metal. The result is that as soon as the laser is no longer directed toward the pool, the heat dissipates into the surrounding region and the pool solidifies.

The speed with which a laser weld can be formed has two important implications. First, lasers can weld seams with amazing rapidity. In a sheet of steel a millimeter thick, for example, a CO_2 laser can weld a seam at the rate of 10 meters per minute, much faster than more traditional methods with a concomitant improvement in production rates. Second, because different types of metals conduct heat at very different rates, welding disparate metals together using traditional methods has often proved difficult. Copper, for example, conducts heat at about 10 times the rate of carbon steel, so welding steel onto copper using conventional techniques has proved quite difficult. Heat dissipates much more quickly on one side of the weld than the other. But even in copper, heat conduction happens at a very slow rate compared to the speed with which energy can be introduced via a laser. As a consequence, welding copper and steel together can be done easily with a laser, because the entire welding process has been completed before much conduction has occurred on either side of the weld.

Laser welding is now common in a variety of industrial applications. In some of those applications—welding automobile frames, for example—it has displaced more conventional forms of welding, but in other applications—welding two disparate metals together, for example—it has made processes commonplace that were once difficult or impossible to perform with more conventional implements.

LASERS IN COMMUNICATION

One of the most important applications of laser technology has developed in the field of communications. Gordon Gould understood this in a way that none of his contemporaries did, and he suggested the use of lasers as communication devices in his original patent application. But lasers are not necessary for communication. Engineers used *electromagnetic waves* for communication long before the invention of the laser. One can employ electromagnetic waves of any frequency for the purpose of communication, and there is a long history of inventors and engineers doing just that. Early in his career, Guglielmo Marconi (1874–1937), the Italian inventor of radio telegraphy, successfully sent messages between Ireland and Argentina using radio waves with *wavelengths* of about eight kilometers. In the years immediately following World War I, Marconi successfully experimented with so-called shortwave radio, electromagnetic waves with wavelengths that are measured in tens of meters.

Communication still occurs at shortwave and at very long wavelengths. The U.S. government, for example, has made use of very long radio waves to communicate with submarines, and international broadcasters such as Radio Netherlands, the Dutch International Service, and many amateur radio operators continue to routinely broadcast on

Artist's conception of NASA's proposed "Mars Laser Communication Demonstration."
Laser-based communication technology promises much faster rates of data transfer
than are currently possible. [NASA]

shortwave frequencies. Despite this activity, the general trend has been
to use electromagnetic waves of ever shorter wavelengths for purposes
of communication. Even Marconi, toward the end of his life, was using
radio waves with a wavelength of about half a meter. The reason is
simple: The shorter the wavelength, the more information that can be
transmitted in a given time, and lasers are valuable, in part, because
the wavelengths of visible light are billions of times shorter than those
Marconi first employed.

Transmitting information on a beam of light, however, introduces
certain unique difficulties. A beam of light is more easily interrupted
than a radio wave. Leaves and clouds, for example, can interrupt a beam
of light; leaves are opaque, and clouds scatter the resulting beam. Light
waves travel in straight lines, and so even when no obstacle is apparent,
the curve of Earth's surface prevents one from transmitting very far.
Nor is this the only difficulty associated with using light to communi-

cate. Engineers have also had to find ways of modulating light, which is another way of saying that they had to learn how to encode information on a beam of light. Overcoming these challenges and harnessing light, especially laser light, for the purpose of communications has had a profound impact on modern life. Amazingly, light was first used as a medium of communication more than 125 years ago.

Bell's Great Invention

The Scottish-born American Alexander Graham Bell (1847–1922) is best remembered as the inventor of the telephone, but his interests and accomplishments ranged far beyond one of history's most important communications innovations. The only interest that he maintained throughout his life involved the education of the deaf. He was an audiologist and an educational theorist. He founded a school for teachers of the deaf and a small experimental school for deaf children. His mother and wife were deaf, and his original concept for the telephone was as a device to assist the hard of hearing. In fact, in 1886, in testimony before the Royal Commission of the United Kingdom on the Condition of the Blind, the Deaf and Dumb, he characterized his work on the telephone as a distraction, something that took his attention away from his work on behalf of the deaf. With respect to his work as an inventor, he held patents on a wide variety of devices, including hydroplanes and the phonograph. He was indefatigable.

Alexander Graham Bell, Scottish-born, American inventor (1847–1922). Bell had successfully found a way to transmit an audio signal on a beam of light by 1880. [SSPL/The Image Works]

By Bell's own estimation, one of his most significant accomplishments was his invention in 1880 of the photophone, a device

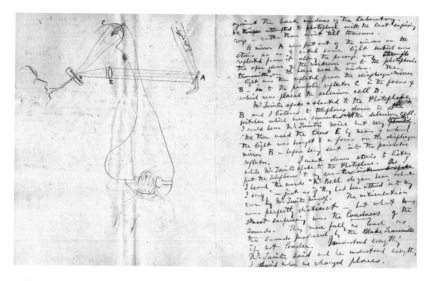

Bell's own illustration of the photophone. The Sun's rays are captured by the mirror at A, concentrated by a lens at E, modulated by the speaker's voice at B, and then reflected toward a parabolic reflector at C. The light signal is converted into an electrical signal at D, which drives the listener's headphones. [Library of Congress, Manuscript Division]

that transmitted the speaker's voice on a beam of light. This device illustrates the basic ideas behind using light as a communications medium, and its shortcomings show why this type of communication did not become widely used until after the invention of the laser.

Bell used sunlight to transmit information. The electric lightbulb was invented only about a year before Bell invented the photophone, and early bulbs were not bright enough for him to use. Bell had two separate and significant design problems to overcome: He had to find a way to modulate, or encode, information about the speaker's voice on the Sun's rays, and he had to find a way to recover this information at the receiver. His solutions, which are simple in concept, help to illustrate how lasers have sometimes been used to perform the same task.

First, Bell needed sunlight with which to work, and so he and his research assistant, Charles Sumner Tainter, placed a silvered mirror outside a window to reflect sunlight toward the device that *modulated* the beam. (In letters to his wife, Bell describes the frustration he and Tainter felt when a cloud passed in front of the Sun, abruptly terminating an experiment.) The sunlight passed through a lens that focused the incoming light on a device that modulated the intensity of the light. Modulation was accomplished by first constructing two screens with numerous identical, narrow slits. These screens were installed so that one screen could move relative to the other. When the slits on the two screens were aligned, light passed through the pair of screens with maximum intensity. Bell and Tainter attached one of the screens to a device that caused it to vibrate in sympathy with the voice. As it vibrated, the slits in one screen moved with respect to the other, and this movement prevented some of the sunlight from passing through. In this way, they varied, or modulated, the intensity of the sunlight in a way that carried information about the speaker's voice.

Next, the modulated sunlight was directed by mirror toward the receiver. This was the part of which Bell was most proud: He had found a way to transmit a signal on a beam of light. All that remained was to convert the modulated sunlight back into an intelligible, audible signal. To do this, they depended on a piece of selenium, a chemical element whose electrical resistance changes when it is exposed to light. Tainter had found that, when processed correctly, the electrical resistance of selenium dropped precipitously when exposed to bright light and increased as soon as the light dimmed. Bell and Tainter used a battery to send a current through the selenium. As the modulated sunlight impinged upon the selenium, the resistance of the circuit of which the selenium was a part varied according to the amount of light that shone on the selenium. The electrical current rose and fell in response to changes in the resistance. Bell simply placed a telephone receiver in the circuit, and from out of the telephone's speaker came (at least sometimes) the voice of the sender.

They tested it by placing the telephone receiver far enough away from the transmitter so that the person at the receiver could not hear the sender. In a letter to his wife, Mabel, Bell described one experiment that he and Tainter performed in the following words:

> I went downstairs to listen while Mr. Tainter spoke to the Photophone. As I put the Telephone to my ear—I heard the words "Mr. Bell do you hear what I say" just as if they had been uttered into my ear by Mr. Tainter himself. The articulation was perfectly clear—but what was most surprising was the loudness of the sounds.

While Bell also writes that not all of the experiments were as successful, he clearly held out great hope for the device, but the invention never found any practical application. One reason is that Bell decided to jealously guard the design of the actual mechanism, which he believed to be one of his greatest scientific accomplishments, in order to protect his rights to it. Second, Bell's device modulated incoherent light, and even under the best of conditions incoherent light spreads out and loses its intensity fairly quickly, which explains why, in practice, his device was limited to very short-range communications. Third, the intensity of the light Bell used to transmit his messages could be no greater than the amount of light originally reflected off the mirror outside the window— not a great deal of light even under the best of conditions. He could have tried to make a much bigger mirror, but then the problem of constructing and aiming the mirror would have been far more difficult. Finally, although Bell seems to have believed that the ability of the photophone to transmit between two points without wires and through the open air was an important advantage, he was wrong. Light is easily absorbed, scattered, and obstructed in the open air. In the open air, Bell's invention could never have worked the way he hoped. A practical implementation of Bell's ideas would not be available until the invention of the laser.

Modulating the Laser

Bell would have had much better results from his photophone had he had access to a laser beam. A laser beam is much more intense than ordinary sunlight, and it remains focused over much longer distances. Recall from chapter 2 that lasers convert electrical energy, whether from a wall outlet or battery, into light energy, so one can vary the intensity of the laser light by simply varying the energy supplied to the laser. Laser light is sometimes modulated in just this way. The voice signal is converted into an electrical signal by a microphone. The electrical signal is used to modulate the power supplied to the laser, and the result is a laser beam that varies in intensity according to the vocal input received by the microphone. While it would be incorrect to describe such a device as "simple," it is "simple enough" that some hobbyists with an interest in lasers have constructed transmitters that modulate the intensity of the laser beam in just this way, and they have used their transmitters to send their voices hundreds or even thousands of feet. But eventually the light begins to spread; it is scattered by dust and other particulate matter in the atmosphere, and the result is that the signal is no longer coherent. Even with a laser there are limits to the transmission of information through open air.

For most contemporary applications, however, lasers are generally modulated in ways that are quite different from that used by Bell. One very specific example is described here. It is a representative method of modulating a laser beam. The precise implementation of the scheme described here actually varies somewhat from one design to the next. This one is taken from a paper entitled "The Power Spectrum of Pulse Position Modulation with Dead Time and Pulse Jitter" by Vilnrotter, Simon, and Yan. The following method of modulating the laser beam has a number of properties in common with other such techniques for encoding digital information on a laser. The name of the scheme is *pulse-position modulation* (PPM). It is, as its name implies, accomplished by using a pulsed laser. The laser beam is modulated by pulsing it on and off according to a very precisely determined scheme.

Our PPM scheme works by dividing the message into "words," which may consist of an actual word but more likely consists of a numerical digit or some other smaller unit of information. Each word is transmitted in the same amount of time. With a *Q-switched* laser, a reasonable amount of time might be 20 microseconds (μs) per word. Recall that Q-switched lasers are capable of brief and powerful bursts of light, and that 1 μs means 1 millionth of a second. Using words of length 20 μs means that 50,000 words can be transmitted each second. Next, the 20-μs time interval is further divided. For example, during one 20-μs time interval, one might allocate an approximately 15-μs period of uninterrupted "dead air," during which time no signal is transmitted. This 15-μs time period is used to separate successive words. Without the dead air, the receiver might be unable to determine where one word ended and the next word began. The remaining 5 μs are then divided into 256 equal time intervals of length 20 nanoseconds (ns). One nanosecond equals 1 billionth of a second, and because computers work in base 2, the PPM scheme works most efficiently when the number of such subintervals is a power of 2. In this case, $256 = 2^8$.

So far the scheme has specified only how the time devoted to an arbitrary word is divided. The next step is to transmit a word by emitting a pulse with the laser. In a standard PPM scheme, the laser is fired only one time per word, and the pulse is limited to one of the 256 time slots of 20 ns apiece. In other words, the laser is fired exactly once during one 20-ns time interval, and it is fired in such a way that the duration of the pulse is less than 20 ns. (Remember that everything that happens with lasers happens very quickly, and the extraordinarily small time intervals involved are still long enough so that there is time for all the processes involved in creating a laser beam to occur.)

The actual pulse is substantially less than the 20 μs. Instead, the laser might fire for approximately 10 ns in the middle of the 20-ns

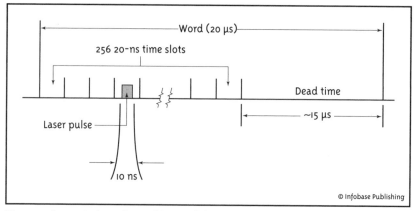

Diagram of a particular pulse-position modulation scheme. Notice that although microsecond (20 μs) intervals are reserved for each "word," the laser fires only for about 10 nanoseconds (ns), or less than one thousandth of the total time allocated for each word.

time interval. The remaining time—approximately 5 ns on each side of pulse—is used as a safety factor. If the duration of a pulse were to extend into an adjoining time interval, there would be ambiguity about the pulse's meaning. Which word did it signify? Did the laser fire too early or did it fire at the right time but last too long? The situation is not immediately clear. These safety intervals on each side of the 10 ns pulse are necessary because the behavior of the laser is just slightly unpredictable over such brief time intervals. The reason for the unpredictability is that there is a little randomness involved in the amount of time necessary to build up a population inversion, just as there is a little randomness involved in how long it will take a laser beam to form after the Q-switch is "thrown" and the resonant properties of the laser cavity are restored. To prevent these uncertainties from interfering with communication, each pulse should lie inside the interval to which it belongs. See the illustration above.

It is an interesting fact that with this particular scheme, the laser is off during almost the entire transmission. Over the course of one minute, for example, during which time it will transmit 50,000 words, the laser is on for a total of 3/100 of a second and is off for 59 97/100 seconds. In other words, it has a duty cycle of one to 2,000. Finally, as each pulse is detected at the receiver, it is reformulated into the appropriate string of zeroes and ones, and the transmitted message is reconstructed.

There are various common modifications of this scheme. First, as with so many other laser applications, the time intervals that determine the word depend, in part, on the length of the wavelength of the electromagnetic waves emitted by the laser. Pulsed lasers with shorter wavelengths can emit shorter pulses than lasers with longer wavelengths, and so all other things being equal, very high frequency lasers can be used to transmit more information per second than lasers that emit electromagnetic waves with longer wavelengths. Second, one can transmit more information by making better use of the numerous "empty" 20 ns time intervals. If one can fire the laser only once per word, then there are 256 possible times in which the laser can be fired, and so there exist only 256 different words that can be expressed by this scheme. (Keep in mind that the term *word* does not mean the type of word found in a dictionary but rather a more basic unit of information.) If, however, the laser is allowed to fire two distinct pulses per word, then the number of different words that can be supported by this scheme rises to 32,640. Modulation schemes that involve multiple pulses per word are called multipulse pulsed-position modulation (MPPM) schemes. Finally, the long (approximately 15 μs) silence incorporated into each word can be shortened (or even eliminated) depending upon the modulation scheme employed and the needs of the user.

Pulsed modulation schemes are preferred to the method of modulation used by Alexander Graham Bell, which involves varying the intensity of the light, because in addition to transmitting the information—and information exchange is, after all, the reason transmissions are initiated—pulsed modulation schemes are also usually designed to include information about the actual sequence of pulses used to represent the information. This type of information is important because the individual at the receiver does not really know what was sent, only what was received. (If the receiver knew what was sent independently of what was received, then there would be no point in sending the transmission since no information was exchanged.) As a consequence, if there is an error either in transmitting or receiving the sequence of pulses, the receiver cannot recognize the existence of such an error without this additional error identification information. Furthermore, with enough additional information encoded into the message, the receiver will also be able to reconstruct the original message *even in the presence of errors*. These additional pulses, which are sent interspersed with the original "content words," are included solely to enable the receiver to identify and correct errors. There is an entire branch of knowledge devoted to the creation of such "error correction codes," and their existence enables the user to transfer large amounts of information through space or along fiber-optic cables, confident in the knowledge that the message that is received is, in fact, identical with the message sent.

Fiber Optics

As previously mentioned, in order to communicate reliably over long distances with a beam of light, one cannot simply shine the light through the atmosphere. Too many impurities will disrupt the beam—fog, insects, dust—almost anything that is visible. A great variety of invisible things can serve to scatter, absorb, or reflect laser light. Once a laser beam has been modulated to carry information, it must be transmitted along a "laser friendly" medium, one that minimizes disruptions to the beam itself. This is the role of fiber optic cable.

Fiber-optic cable is to lasers what plumbing is to water. It provides a path by which light can travel for fairly long distances without disruption. Fiber-optic cable is a conduit for light, or more generally,

Workers laying fiber-optic cable in downtown Austin, Texas. Fiber-optic technology has made it possible to transfer streams of data virtually error-free and at rates that far exceed those of previous technologies. (Bob Daemmrich/The Image Works)

a conduit for a somewhat larger class of electromagnetic waves that includes visible light. It is a purely passive medium that protects the modulated wave inside it.

Ordinary glass, the type of glass used in windows, for example, is something that is usually characterized as transparent, but it is not nearly transparent enough for optical fiber, which is an extraordinary technical achievement. Optical fiber is often created in continuous lengths of 7.5 miles (12 km). Theoretically speaking, there is no reason why it could not be made in even longer lengths, but the spools on which the cable is stored would become too large and unwieldy. The material out of which the fiber is created is extremely pure. It is so pure that it is easily possible to shine a laser of the right wavelength in one end and have it emerge 7.5 miles (12 km) down at the other end almost as bright as it entered—"almost" because any signal degrades somewhat as it travels between sender and receiver. This is true whether it is an electrical signal transmitted along a copper wire, a radio wave transmitted through space, or a laser beam transmitted along a fiber optic cable. But fiber-optic cable is currently the best of all mediums through which to transmit light. In practice, the 7.5-mile (12-km) lengths of cable are joined to produce much longer pathways, and the initial signal is conveyed through these longer pathways. The signal may require no amplification until it has traveled more than 62 miles (100 km) of fiber. Eventually, however, even the clearest signal transmitted over the best cable will become weak. Amplifiers are installed at strategic points along the fiber-optic pathways to retransmit a stronger version of the received signal. In this way, the signal is preserved until it reaches its destination.

While the technology involved in producing modern fiber-optic filament is extremely complex, the concepts on which it is based are relatively straightforward. First, the material out of which the filament is constructed must be as pure as possible. Second, the fiber must contain the light. Unless the cable is properly built, light can escape because the light rays must necessarily impinge on the sides of the fiber as it twists up and down and around corners.

The key to confining the light within the fiber lies in manipulating a characteristic of the materials out of which the fiber is made; that characteristic is called the index of refraction. Recall from chapter 1 that light travels through a vacuum at 186,000 miles per second (300,000 km/s). But in other materials, air or water, for example, light travels more slowly. The index of refraction for a particular material is a fraction formed by comparing the speed of light in a vacuum to the speed of light in the material in question. This is the formula:

$$index\ of\ refraction\ for\ given\ material = \frac{speed\ of\ light\ in\ a\ vacuum}{speed\ of\ light\ in\ the\ material}$$

Because light is at its fastest in a vacuum, the index of refraction is always a number that is greater than or equal to one. For purposes of illustration, the index of refraction in air is 1.0003, which shows that light travels through air almost as fast as it travels through a vacuum. Light in water is considerably slower, with an index of refraction of 1.33.

Now suppose that two transparent materials are placed side by side. Suppose further that the materials have different indices of refraction. If a ray of light is propagating through the material with the larger index of refraction—that is, it is propagating through the slower of the two pathways—then when it strikes the boundary between the two materials it will be reflected back inside the material with the larger index of refraction, provided that the angle at which it strikes the material is not too steep. In other words, as long as it is a "glancing blow" the light will remain inside the material with the larger index of refraction.

Fiber-optic cable actually consists of two materials, a core material and a cladding or shielding material. The core material has a slightly larger index of refraction (1.48) than the cladding (1.46). The small

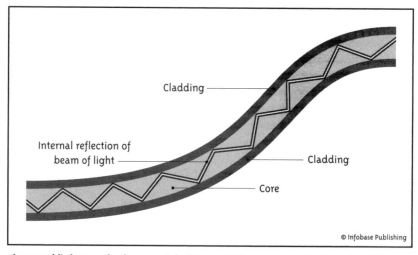

© Infobase Publishing

The ray of light travels along straight lines until it encounters the boundary between the core and the cladding, at which point it is reflected back into the core.

difference between the two indices of refraction ensures that the light remains confined to the core as long as the cable is not bent too sharply. These two relatively simple physical principles, purity of material and maintaining the difference in the index of refraction between the core and cladding, enable light to be successfully transmitted over fairly long distances.

Fiber-optic cable is insensitive to the light source, and other sources besides lasers are used to transmit light along the cable. Currently, lasers and light-emitting diodes (LEDs), the tiny brilliant lights often used on the controls of many stereo systems, are used to transmit signals along fiber-optic cables. The wavelength of the lasers used is either 1.310 micrometers (μm) or 1.550 μm. The LEDs emit light with wavelengths of 850 nanometers and 1.300 μm. (Notice that the laser wavelengths are in the infrared and so are invisible. But because they can still cause irreparable harm to one's vision, never look into a fiber-optic communications line.)

Fiber-optic cable is of such high quality and low cost—and it can carry so much information—that today all high-capacity communication networks rely on it at some point in the system. Fiber-optic lines are also used to transmit laser light in various industrial and medical applications. It is as important to many applications of lasers as the lasers themselves.

8

READING AND WRITING WITH LASERS

L asers are everywhere. All large stores and many small ones now use lasers to read the *Universal Product Code* (UPC), the pattern of black stripes on a white background found on virtually all consumer goods, in order to speed checkout and to provide input for inventory tracking systems. Lasers are also used in CD and DVD players to read information from discs and to write information onto discs. In laser printers, they enable the user to display electronically stored files on paper.

With respect to UPC labels, CDs, and DVDs, lasers are used to provide input for software programs. They are not used to process information. Instead, they perform a role analogous to eyes. Just as eyes are for looking and brains are for seeing—in the sense that the eyes provide input and the brain provides processing power—lasers enable computers, large and small, to acquire input to analyze. The seeing is done by the computer; the looking is often done with lasers.

In some cases, lasers perform work that could, in theory, be done by humans. The U.S. Postal Service, for example, uses lasers in massive letter-sorting machines to read addresses on envelopes and then sort them accordingly. These machines sort upward of 30,000 letters per hour. The letters are entrained by rapidly moving belts and passed through the machine so fast that individual envelopes cannot be identified by eye. The mail stream looks like a long white ribbon. While one can imagine doing this work by hand—in fact, at one time it was done by hand—the volume of mail currently handled by the Postal Service would make it impossible to hire enough staff.

Other tasks can probably be done only by lasers. The information on a CD, for example, was created with lasers in mind: One can inspect the bumps on the surface of a CD with a microscope and in the process observe the information contained therein, but reading this information by eye is simply not possible because of the format and density with which it is stored. Reading the information requires the use of a laser.

Whether the information in a certain type of media is accessible to the human eye or not, lasers have often proved indispensable in accessing it. Notice, for example, that incandescent light, while useful to people, is seldom if ever used by any of the machines described in the preceding paragraph. The questions of how lasers accomplish their tasks, and why laser light, as opposed to ordinary, incoherent light, is employed by the engineers who designed these machines, illustrates some important properties of lasers as well as their uses.

UPCs

Universal Product Code (UPC) is the square design one finds on the sides of cans, bags, and boxes of food consisting of black vertical thin and thick lines on a white background, and beneath the lines are a set of numbers. The pattern represents the numbers used to identify the type of merchandise to which the code is affixed, the manufacturer, and the particular item. In addition, there is a digit that enables the machine to check to see if it read the other digits correctly. The UPC is an extremely useful invention—so useful, and so important to modern methods of inventory control, that one of the inventors was awarded the National Medal of Technology in 1992. It is also an innovation that depends in an essential way on lasers.

The need for something like the modern-day UPC was recognized at least as early as 1932, when Wallace Flint of Harvard University suggested that consumers order items from catalogs by removing punch cards from the catalogue that identified the goods they wanted to purchase. The punch cards would be used for two purposes: First, the cards would enable the staff to pull the items of interest to the consumer from the shelves where they were stored, and second, the

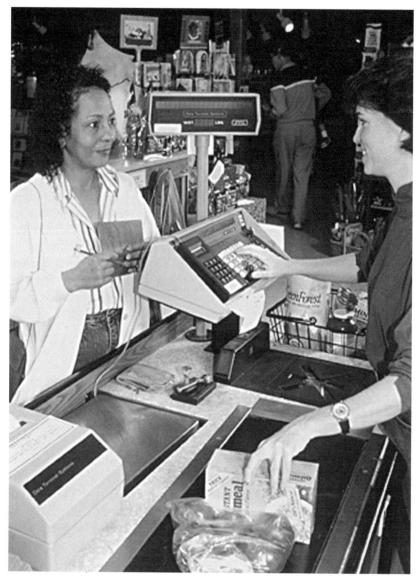

Grocery store checkout. Inventors began experimenting with various versions of the UPC code in the 1930s, but the concept could not be implemented until after the invention of the laser. [Bob Daemmrich/The Image Works]

cards would enable the merchant to keep track of inventory. Punch cards and the machines that read them were, however, ill-suited to the task. The concept proposed by Flint was a valuable one. Conceptually, it is similar to today's UPC, but the technology needed to implement the concept had not yet been developed.

In 1948, independently of Flint, two graduate students at Drexel University, Bernard Silver and Joseph Woodland, began work on developing what would eventually become the UPC. They experimented with circular designs so that the code would scan the same way no matter how it was held, and they tried modifying Morse code: The dots of the code were elongated to form thin lines, and the dashes were elongated to form thick lines. The fundamental difficulty arose when they tried to construct a device to read the code. The device was to consist of two parts, a light sensor and a light source.

The light sensor was constructed from vacuum tubes. It was an extremely crude device by today's standards, but if the pattern were properly illuminated, it could detect it. The light source proved to be the bigger problem. They opted for a 500-watt incandescent bulb. (The laser had not yet been invented.) Like every incandescent bulb, this one generated far more heat than light, and it generated a lot of light. Furthermore, because they used an incandescent bulb, the resulting light was unfocused and incoherent. The bulb was so hot that if one held the paper on which the code was printed too close to it, the paper would begin to smolder. It was an unpromising start, but they made it work. Their device was huge, hot, and expensive, but if a coded piece of paper was held in the right position, the machine could detect the pattern. Their creation was not practical, but practicality is not a requirement for patent protection. Silver and Woodland received a U.S. patent on their invention in 1952.

The UPC system did not become feasible until the 1970s, when microchips and lasers became cheap and reliable. Microchips enabled fast processing and exchange of information, and lasers enabled the designers to efficiently illuminate the code. The idea is simple enough. The white part of the label reflects the laser light more efficiently than the black part, which tends to absorb light. When the code is scanned with the laser—and this is done from a variety of angles many times in one second so that the shop cashier can hold the item at whatever distance and in whatever way is convenient—the pattern of reflected light detected by the machine's sensor identifies the item. The data are processed, and the price and description of the item are displayed to the consumer and cashier. Just as important, the information is also logged into a database so that the merchant can track what is and is not selling.

In the early years of this technology, the most popular laser used for reading UPC codes was the helium neon laser—abbreviated HeNe.

The HeNe laser was also used in early laser printers and to read laser discs, the predecessor to the CD. HeNe lasers are CW, low-output devices that are generally designed to emit red light at a wavelength of 632.8 nanometers (nm), although they can be designed to emit light at other wavelengths. They are durable, not especially expensive, and similar in concept to the CO_2 lasers described in chapter 6.

A standard HeNe laser consists of a sealed tube filled with helium and neon gas at low pressure. The mixture is predominantly helium, often between 70 and 90 percent, and the two-component gas mixture is excited by passing a high-voltage electrical current from one end of the tube to the other. The current excites the helium, which raises the energy of the neon via collisions, and a population inversion is created in the neon. A highly reflective mirror is placed at one end of the tube, and a partially reflective mirror is placed at the other end, positioned so that it is parallel with the opaque mirror. Power is applied; *stimulated emission* occurs; an intense, coherent wave is formed in the resonating cavity; and from the end of the tube shines the familiar, red light of the HeNe laser.

HeNe lasers remain important for other applications because they are a pure source of light and are relatively inexpensive, but they have since been replaced in many of their initial applications, including the reading of UPC codes, by laser diodes. The same very broad principles that govern the production of laser light in other mediums also apply to diode lasers, but the mechanisms employed to produce stimulated emission are quite different in laser diodes as are some of the physical characteristics of these devices, also called semiconductor lasers.

Semiconductors are a class of materials that are used in a wide variety of electronic devices, most famously in computer chips. Scientists have become quite adept at manipulating the chemical composition of these devices so that they can obtain a wide variety of effects. When an electrical current is passed through the types of semiconductors used in computers, for example, some of the electricity is converted into heat, but when the semiconductor is gallium-arsenide, for example, some of the electricity is also converted into laser light.

The first remarkable property of these CW lasers that one notices is their size. They are often no larger than a grain of salt. The ends of the devices are cut—and sometimes polished and coated—to produce a resonant cavity that is similar in concept to what one finds in the HeNe laser, at least in the sense that it is made so that light *oscillates* between the ends to amplify the original impulse via the process of stimulated emission. The sides of the resonant cavity, which are interior to the semiconductor chip, reflect rather than absorb the beam of light because their *index of refraction* (see chapter 7) is higher than that of the tiny region in which the light is produced. When one applies an electrical voltage across the semiconductor, a bright, but not particularly focused, light is produced.

The laser beam that emanates from many of these devices is really more of a roughly shaped laser cone because the cavity in which it is produced is so extremely short that there is not sufficient length to create a narrow beam; nor is the cross section of this cone round. The asymmetries and spreading characteristic of these diode-produced beams can be corrected with the use of lenses. The extra lenses, when they are needed, are generally considered worth the expense and effort because of certain other not-so-obvious properties of these lasers. First, laser diodes are extremely efficient. In a well-made laser diode more than 50 percent of the electricity applied to the laser is converted into laser light. These laser diodes are the most efficient light source currently known. (Calculations indicate that laser diodes with efficiencies of 80 percent are possible.) Recall that some optically *pumped* ruby lasers are less than 1 percent efficient, and an ordinary incandescent lightbulb converts from 5 to 10 percent of the electricity it consumes into light, with the rest of the electricity converted into heat. Laser diode efficiency makes them ideal for use in low power applications; they are the laser light source of choice for any battery-powered device, including the ubiquitous laser pointer, or where the high voltages characteristic of HeNe lasers are simply undesirable, in consumer electronics, for example.

Finally, laser diodes are extremely long-lived and can be constructed to emit light at a variety of *wavelengths*. The laser diodes used to read UPC symbols generally emit light at 670 nm and so appear slightly redder than the light emitted by their predecessor, the HeNe laser, which emits light at 632.8 nm. Although their light is easy to see, and virtually everyone has seen laser light produced by these semiconductors, the lasers themselves are sometimes best viewed with a magnifying glass.

CDs and DVDs

The problems the designers of compact discs (CDs) and digital versatile discs or digital video discs (DVDs) faced are the exact opposite of those faced by the designers of UPC readers. A UPC code holds very

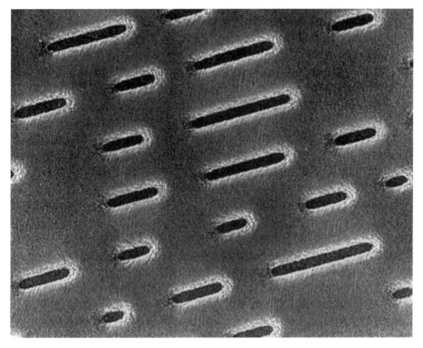

Surface of a compact disc (CD) magnified 3,500 times. [Dr. Dennis Kunkel/Visuals Unlimited]

little information. Though the information is extremely important to both the consumer and the merchant, each UPC code consists only of a small number of digits. One of the main challenges faced by designers of UPC readers is that there is a great deal of uncertainty about the distance from the reader that the code will be held and a great deal of uncertainty about the orientation of the code in three-dimensional space. By contrast, there is little uncertainty about how a CD or DVD will be placed with respect to the laser scanner used to read them. Additionally, these media contain a great deal of information in contrast to the UPC.

To understand the principles on which CDs and DVDs are designed, it may help to keep in mind that information has been stored on discs for about a century. The first phonographs used cylinders, which stored a few minutes' worth of music or speech. Inventors immediately began to search for ways of storing more information. Because long before consumers measured information transfer speeds in bits per second, there was an insatiable demand for storage media with higher information capacity and quicker transfer rates. The 78 rpm disc gave way to the long-playing (LP) disc, and monophonic, or single channel, recordings gave way to stereo.

The next major step was to store information on discs digitally. The result was the CD, a device that did not become widely available until reliable laser diodes could be produced relatively inexpensively. The first generation of these lasers emitted light in the infrared, and so more or less by accident a standard was born. To this day, CD players use lasers that emit light at 780 nanometers (nm). The wavelength of the laser used to read information on a disc is important, because the shorter the wavelength, the more densely information can be stored.

Information is stored on a CD in the form of small holes, called pits. For a read-only disc, the pits are made by ablating, or vaporizing, tiny craterlike holes. This is why the CD is read-only: One cannot replace the material that has been vaporized. For CD-RW discs, the pits are made in a different way. (The details are omitted here.) What is important is that the minimum size of the pits that the device can read is determined by the wavelength of the laser used to read them—the longer the wavelength, the larger the minimum size of the pits. In the case of CDs, the pits are 1.6 micrometers (μm) in diameter. Even at 1.6 μm, however, the laser reader has a hard time reading a single pit. As a result, designers developed a method of data storage called EFM, which is short for "eight to fourteen modulation."

The modulation scheme works by converting the data, which is initially stored in bytes, units consisting of eight bits, to a 14-bit scheme. (A single bit can be pictured as either a one or zero.) There are 256 different eight-bit words, but naively storing them on the disc as ones and zeros—for example, letting a single pit represent a one, and a single untouched space, called a "land," represent a zero—led to problems with data retrieval, because, as previously mentioned, the sensor had difficulty reading such tiny structures. Instead, designers decided to first reexpress each (eight-bit) byte as a 14-bit sequence of ones and zeros. There are 32,756 possible 14-bit words, and only 256 of them are actually needed. Only 14-bit sequences with the following property are used: Each pair of ones is separated by at least two but no more than 10 zeros.

This is a purely conceptual device: It is a way of picturing what they actually burn onto the CD as a sequence of pits and lands. The way the 14-bit sequence is represented on the disc is as follows: The pits and lands are placed on the disc in a spiral pattern so that they can be read one after the other in an unambiguous way. When the laser hits a flat spot, whether it is a land or a pit, the light is reflected up to the sensor, and the input is assigned a zero. When the sensor detects a jump up (from pit to land) or a jump down (from land to pit), the input is assigned a value of one. The result is the 14-digit code described earlier. The restriction of at least two and no more than 10 zeros between each one specifies the minimum and maximum length of each pit. In this way, digital information is stored on a disc and then retrieved. (Notice in the accompanying photo that not all pits are of equal length. The length of the pit specifies the number of sequential zeros, at least two but no more than 10.)

CDs are already old, technologically speaking. Their information capacity is too small for storing movies, for example, and this has led

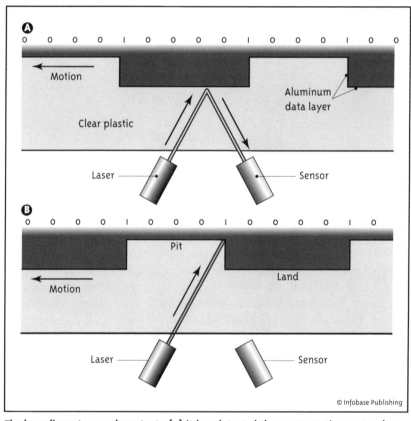

The laser fires at a regular rate. In (a) it has detected three consecutive spots where a change in height has *not* occurred. These are represented by zeros. In (b) it detects a jump in height from a pit to a land and records a one.

to the creation of DVDs. The difference between DVDs and CDs is conceptually not very great. The first, and from the point of view of this book the most important, difference is that the laser diode used in a DVD has a wavelength of between 635 and 650 nm. DVDs use visible (red) light rather than infrared light to detect pits and lands. A shorter wavelength means that DVD laser scanners can read smaller patterns of pits and lands than are used on a CD, and, indeed, DVD pits are only 0.4 µm in diameter. A higher-frequency laser also means that the patterns of pits and lands can be placed closer together on the disc. As a consequence, the information capacity of DVDs is much larger than that of CDs. (The scheme by which information is encoded on DVDs, called EFM+, is a modification of the EFM scheme used on CDs and described earlier. EFM+ enables a still denser "packing" of information on the surface of the DVD.) The result is an information storage medium that can handle many times more information than the CD.

A new generation of DVDs is being introduced as of this writing that will enable content producers to store even more information, but the real breakthrough will come when engineers find a way to make inexpensive laser diodes that emit light in the blue (or even higher) portion of the electromagnetic *spectrum*. This will result in DVDs that have capacities many times higher than those currently available commercially. The introduction of this next generation of DVDs is only a matter of time and wavelength.

Laser Printers

Printing technology is another application that depends in an essential way on lasers. Laser printers have become relatively inexpensive and are used in many homes and businesses. They are the light of choice because they can be targeted with great precision and so produce a clean, sharply defined image. As with the devices used to read UPCs, the laser of choice early in the development of laser printers was the HeNe laser. When cheap, reliable laser diodes became available, however, HeNe lasers gave way to laser diodes in this application as well. Now essentially all laser printers depend on laser diodes.

To understand how laser printers work, it is first necessary to know about a class of materials called photoconductors. Electrically speaking, most materials fall into one of two classes: They are either conductors—electrical charges flow easily through them—or they are insulators, in which case electrical charges do not flow easily through them. Copper is an example of a conductor. Electricity flows easily through copper, which is why underneath the plastic sheathing that covers most electrical wiring there is a copper core. By contrast, the plastic sheathing itself is an insulator. The electrical charges that enable lights to glow and computers to compute are constrained to flow along the copper core of the wires leading to these devices only because of the insulation that surrounds it. Without the insulation, the electrical charges would flow out of the wire in an uncontrolled way, creating a short circuit.

Under ordinary conditions, the electrical properties of the materials that make up the wire do not change: The copper core is always a conductor, and the plastic sheathing is always an insulator. These are intrinsic properties of these materials. The copper is a conductor even when there are no electrical charges flowing through it, and insulators can have electrically charged surfaces, but because they are insulators, the charges cannot flow through them or across their surfaces. However, there are other materials that fail to conform to such a simple classification scheme. In fact, there is one class of materials, called photoconductors, whose electrical properties depend on whether or not they are illuminated.

Photoconductors are insulators when they are in the dark and conductors when they are in the light. Moreover, if one uses a narrow beam of light—a laser, for example—to illuminate a line on a photoconductor's surface, only the illuminated region will conduct electricity. The rest of the surface will remain an insulator. It is the pairing of a laser with a cylinder to which a photoconductor has been applied that has made the laser printer possible. The procedure consists of five steps.

The first step occurs in the dark. The cylinder, often called a drum, on which a photoconducting material has been applied is rotated beneath a device that "charges the drum," which is another way of saying that electrical charges are distributed evenly across the surface of the cylinder. Because this occurs in the dark, the cylinder's surface is an insulator, and the charges maintain their position.

The second step involves the laser. The computer transfers to the printer information about the pattern to be reproduced. A tightly focused laser beam is directed across the spinning drum with the help of mirrors and with the goal of reproducing the desired image on the surface of the drum. Each point on the drum that is illuminated by the laser changes briefly from an insulator to a conductor, and the electrical charge that was residing there flows away. When the laser is finished with its work, what remains on the drum is a pattern of electrically charged and uncharged regions that—if one could see it—is an image of the pattern that will eventually emerge from the printer on a sheet of paper. (Notice that if the light is not tightly focused—if one used an incandescent light, for example—the stray rays would illuminate other parts of the drum, and the resulting pattern would bear little relationship to the input delivered by the computer.)

Third, toner, which is not ink but an extremely fine plastic powder, is given an electrical charge that is of the same type as that applied to the drum. The toner is then applied to the drum, but it sticks only to those regions that were illuminated by the laser. Why? Like charges repel, and so the toner cannot stick to those parts of the drum that still hold an electrical charge identical to its own.

Fourth, a piece of fresh paper is drawn from the paper tray and given an electrical charge that is opposite to that of the toner that is sticking to the previously illuminated parts of the drum. The result is that the toner is attracted from the drum to the paper, where it adheres, if only weakly, to the paper's surface.

Finally, the paper is subjected to sufficient heat and pressure so that the toner particles are fused permanently to its surface. This last step explains why paper emerging from a laser printer is warm to the touch. (Notice that the role of the laser is to create a pattern on the drum not to supply the heat necessary to fuse the toner to the paper.)

Laser printers are preferred over other designs for their precise copy and for their printing speed. Both these characteristics result from the use of the laser, which can produce extraordinarily detailed patterns at the speed of light.

9

LASERS AS
MEASUREMENT DEVICES

For centuries, linear measurements were made with rulers, surveyor's transits, plumb bobs, and a variety of other similar tools. The results obtained through the skillful use of these simple instruments are remarkable. An array of graceful and monumental buildings, accurate maps, long tunnels, even the gentle, relentlessly straight incline of Roman aqueducts attest to the precision attainable with these implements. The results obtained with these ancient instruments and associated techniques are so accurate that they influenced the designs of many early laser surveying tools.

Consider the problem of measuring a distance. Early surveyors sometimes used the following scheme (see the illustration on page 109): Suppose that the surveyor wants to measure the distance from point A to point B. Suppose further that it is not possible to measure this distance directly. (Perhaps a river lies between the two points.) Instead, the distance from point A to point C is measured directly, and then the angle formed by the two segments AC and BC is measured. With a little trigonometry, one can then compute the distance from A to B. The scheme is simple enough that some early laser-surveying instruments retained some prelaser methods. For example, to measure distances one can place the laser at one end of a bar (position A in the diagram) and place a mirror at the other end of the bar (position C in the diagram). The user will know the length of the bar. This cor-

Using standard trigonometry, one can measure the distance from point *A* to point *B* while remaining on the "*A* side" of the riverbank by making additional measurements from point *C*. Some early laser-based instruments used similar concepts to measure distances.

responds to the distance *AC*, although it is not nearly so far away from the laser as the diagram makes it appear. Next, one rotates the mirror until light from the laser makes a complete circuit, from *A* to *B* to *C* and back to *A*, that is, one aims the laser from *A* to *B* and then rotates the mirror until one can see the laser's "dot" on the other side of the river by looking along the bar toward the mirror. The user notes the angle formed by the bar and the mirror and with a little trigonometry computes the distance from *A* to *C*. Because light travels in straight lines and the light from a laser remains tightly focused over long distances, these types of devices offered modest improvements over nonlaser devices. (No one uses these devices anymore.)

Another type of laser-measurement device makes use of the fact that light travels at constant speed. As a consequence, knowing the time it takes for light to travel from point *A* to point *B* is equivalent to knowing the distance between those points. In a vacuum, light travels at exactly 186,000 miles per second (300,000 km/s), and it travels almost this fast through air. Therefore, if one can measure the time it takes (in seconds) for light to travel from point *A* to point *B*, one may compute *x*, the distance from *A* to *B*, (in kilometers) according to the following extremely simple formula: $300,000t = x$. (Notice that this is essentially a variant of Galileo's method, described in chapter 1.) The difficulty with this method of measuring distances arises because light

Buzz Aldrin Jr. of *Apollo 11*. One of the science packages left behind on this mission was a device called a Laser Ranging Retro-Reflector—shown here situated between the device in the foreground and the American flag in the background—whose purpose was to reflect laser beams from Earth back toward Earth. [NASA]

travels so quickly that measuring *t* can be a technical challenge, but it was not long after the invention of the first laser that scientists had found a way to obtain reasonably accurate measurements for *t* for a variety of situations. Again, although the use of lasers to accomplish this task was new, this type of measurement was a straightforward extension of known concepts. It was a nice accomplishment, but not a surprising one.

From a practical point of view much of the value of laser-based devices lies in their ability to rapidly make many millions, even billions, of accurate measurements rather than as an alternative method of making a single measurement. The creation of these high-output devices is something new. They can produce avalanches of data at rates that no

19th- or early 20th-century surveyor or scientist could have foreseen. These devices have made it possible to create accurate, highly detailed, three-dimensional representations of complex surfaces.

Lasers as Surveying Tools

One of the most spectacular applications of lasers to the problem of surveying involves the use of *lidar*, an acronym for "light detecting and ranging." Lidar works in a way that is analogous to radar but uses light rather than the longer wavelength *electromagnetic waves* characteristic of radar. In its simplest form lidar works as follows: The laser emits a brief pulse. The reflection is detected by a sensor. The time that elapsed between the firing of the laser and the detection of the reflection is used to compute the distance. So far it seems identical to the scheme described in the previous section. The differences arise in the way that it is used.

Lidar is now used to generate detailed maps of shorelines in order to monitor erosion; it is used to produce precise topographical maps to assist in modeling the possible effects of flooding; it has been used to generate maps of the forest canopy in ecological studies. Maps like these require an enormous number of data points to create. To acquire the information necessary to produce these maps, measurements are taken from an airplane. The lidar is mounted so that the laser can be fired from the underside of the plane. In order to cover large areas, the laser must be fired rapidly in many directions, but the laser itself does not turn. Instead, a mirror is mounted below the laser to direct the beam in a predetermined pattern. These are often *Q-switched* lasers that fire anywhere from a few thousand to tens of thousands of very brief bursts of light per second. Despite the relatively high rate of pulsing, these lasers have a low duty cycle, that is, they are off most of the time. During the down time, the sensor detects the reflections of the previous pulse. There is sufficient time for all of this to occur because the speed of light is so fast compared with the time it takes to travel from the plane to the target and because the laser emits such brief pulses.

Real targets are seldom smooth, and so they seldom generate a simple reflection. When flying over a forest, for example, part of the laser beam may reflect off a leaf, part may reflect off branches farther down, and a third reflection may be generated by the ground. In fact, the ground may be the fourth or fifth reflection received by the sensor. The assumption is that the last reflection to arrive at the sensor represents information about the distance of the laser to the ground. For this reason, some modern lidar systems are programmed to detect multiple reflections between individual laser pulses. The

September 9, 1994. The payload on this launch is the Lidar InSpace Technology Experiment (LITE), an early attempt to use lidar techniques from low Earth orbit. It is carried into space by the shuttle *Discovery.* [Courtesy NASA]

Laser survey instrument setup north of Mount Saint Helens, August 6, 1980. This is a highly accurate technology that enables the user to measure changes on the slope from a safe distance. [M. Lukk and the U.S. Geological Service]

multiple reflections associated with each pulse enable ecologists, for example, to generate a topographical map of the forest floor while simultaneously generating a map of the forest canopy. The first reflection received yields the height of the tree, the last the elevation of the ground.

Lidar measurements by themselves, however, do not contain sufficient information to create a map. The reason is simple: The measurements obtained by a lidar system enable the user to determine the distance of a given point to the laser, but in this case the laser is continuously moving. To make the measurements meaningful, the plane's flight path must be taken into consideration as well as uncertainties about the plane's true elevation as well as its latitude and longitude at the time of each measurement. Without detailed information on the position of the laser in three-dimensional space, the data generated by the lidar system has no meaning. To address this issue, the plane is also equipped with a global positioning system (GPS). GPS is a technology that uses satellites and radio waves to determine one's position on Earth. Lidar systems use the same sort of GPS technology that is found in cars and consumer electronics stores, except that lidar GPS systems are more sophisticated. These state-of-the-art devices can identify one's position on Earth's surface with an uncertainty of only a few millimeters. By equipping the plane with a GPS device—and by measuring the position of the GPS device relative to the laser—one can generate millions of highly accurate measurements by flying over the terrain of interest, but even this is not enough. The system is further supplemented by a device called an inertial navigation system (INS), which supplements information about the position of the laser obtained from the GPS with information about its orientation in three-dimensional space as it generates pulses. This information is necessary to determine whether the laser is pointing northeast, south-west, straight down, and so on. (The laser's orientation can change as the plane banks into a turn or as it encounters turbulence.)

As usual, the performance of the system is highly dependent on the *wavelength* of the laser employed. For applications that involve mea-surements over forested areas, for example, designers often use lasers with infrared wavelengths between 900 and 1,064 nanometers (nm). At these wavelengths, vegetation is highly reflective, which ensures robust input for the lidar sensor. By contrast, light in the visible part of the *spectrum* is largely absorbed by vegetation. When airborne lidar systems are used to penetrate shallow bodies of water, wavelengths of approximately 532 nm work better. (This is green light.)

Lasers in Earth Science

Another measurement problem in which lasers have proved useful involves the detection of very small changes in very large objects. Sci-entists have long known that Earth's crust is in continual motion. It is fragmented into a number of irregularly shaped pieces called tectonic plates, which slowly scrape past one another and occasionally collide. These motions make themselves manifest in the form of earthquakes, but the rate at which the motions of these plates affect most surface features is harder to ascertain. Over very long periods of time the effects are obvious: Mountain ranges, which are the result of plate collisions, form along the boundaries of colliding plates. Meanwhile, other features pull apart as the plates on which they are located careen about Earth's surface in extraordinarily slow motion. In fact, most geo-logic features change too slowly to be perceptible, even over the course of many lifetimes. To determine the relative velocities of neighboring plates, or the rate at which a mountain continues to grow, geologists need devices that are sufficiently sensitive to measure the motion of one landmass with respect to another especially when the changes are tiny compared to the size of the landmasses.

Sometimes the problem is simple. If a laser and a reflector can be set up within sight of each other, the problem reduces to firing the laser at the reflector and measuring the time it takes for the signal to make the round-trip. Because the speed of light is known, the distance between the two points is simply the elapsed time divided by two—to take into account the fact that the signal travels back and forth to reach the sensor—and then multiplied by the speed of light. Notice, again, that this is also simply a more sophisticated variant of the experiment Galileo performed during the Renaissance.

The real difficulty arises when one wants to measure the distance between two points, A and B, when B is not visible from A. This might occur when they are positioned on opposite sides of a mountain, for example, or when they are positioned so far apart that the curve of Earth's surface obscures the view. Because light travels in a straight line, if the two points are not in each other's line of sight, light emitted

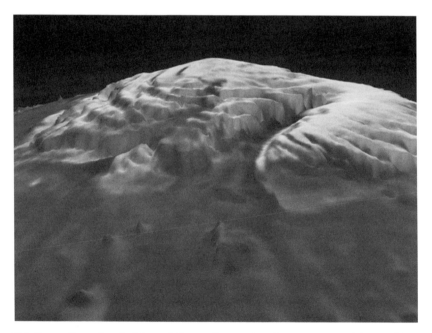

This three-dimensional picture of the Martian north pole was generated from orbit, using approximately 2.6 million laser pulses. It has a spatial resolution of one kilometer and a vertical accuracy of five to 30 meters. [NASA]

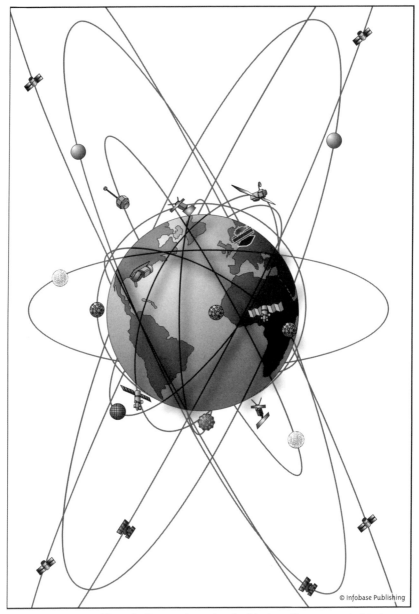

There are many satellites circling Earth outfitted with the reflectors needed to be targets for satellite laser ranging.

at *A* will not reach *B*, and another technique must be used. One solution is to use a technique called satellite laser ranging (SLR). The goal is to measure small changes in position in any direction, north-south, east-west, or vertically. The concept involves using satellites and lasers to first ascertain one's position and then to detect changes with future measurements.

The description should by now seem familiar. One needs reflecting targets, and in this case that means a collection of satellites, each of which is equipped with an array of quartz reflectors attached to their surface. The orientation of each satellite relative to the surface of Earth is carefully stabilized in order to provide as predictable a target as possible. A common choice for a laser is the Nd:YAG, because it is stable and, properly designed, can fire very short pulses. (Recall that Nd:YAG lasers emit an infrared beam at a wavelength of 1,064 nm.) To better penetrate the atmosphere, however, the laser beam is passed through a device that causes the frequency of the wave to double. As described in chapter 1, when the frequency doubles, the wavelength is cut in half, and so the wavelength of the light that is directed at the satellite is 532 nm, exactly half the wavelength of the original beam. (This technique of frequency doubling is commonly applied to the relatively inexpensive and easy-to-control Nd:YAG and results in a green beam.) For safety reasons, the laser emits a low-power beam. Early versions of this technology had the laser firing only a few times per second, but this soon changed. (In science one can never know less by measuring more.) Large numbers of measurements can be better analyzed statistically, and so current SLR systems have lasers that fire about 2,000 times per second. The length of a pulse is measured in picoseconds or trillionths of a second. (The word *picosecond* is abbreviated ps, so that 1 s = 1,000,000,000,000 ps.) One version of SLR laser emits a pulse length of 10 ps. Because the laser is fired 2,000 times per second, this means that it has a duty cycle of 2:10,000,000. It is off virtually all of the time.

The final problem involves detecting the reflection. To accomplish this, the sensor placed by the laser is equipped with a clock that can discriminate between signals that are separated by a little more than one picosecond. This is important because when the laser is fired at a satellite in a high orbit, where a high orbit is measured in thousands of miles, at a rate of 2,000 pulses per second, there may be as many as a few hundred pulses in transit—that is, these pulses are either traveling toward the satellite or back toward the sensor—at any given instant. The time at which the pulse is emitted and the time at which it returns must be carefully measured, otherwise it is not possible to determine which return signal is associated with which emitted pulse. In particular, it is not possible to simply count the pulses going out and comparing them with reflections returning—not at least in the sense that the 100th reflection detected necessarily represents the 100th pulse emitted. Keep in mind that for safety reasons the lasers are not very powerful and that their targets are relatively small. As a result, in the case of a satellite in a higher orbit, the reflected pulse might consist of a single *photon*. The signal could not be any weaker, and as a result sometimes a reflection is not detected at all. Consequently, the timing of the signal is measured as precisely as possible and then the measured value compared with the predicted value. Finally, the result is compared with the last 1,000 measurements in order to determine which reflection is associated with which pulse. With so many measurements and such sophisticated technology, it is possible to detect shifts in the position of the laser of less than a millimeter. The result is that scientists can observe the motion of the continents across Earth's surface as well as the rise and fall of mountains even when they are moving only very short distances.

Lasers in Astronomy

One of the first, and still the most famous, application of lasers in the field of astronomy involved measuring the Earth-Moon distance to within several centimeters by measuring the round-trip time of a laser pulse. The laser was on Earth, and the reflector was on the Moon, left there by Apollo astronauts. The technology involved is the same as that used in the previous two sections.

Another, perhaps more novel, use of lasers in astronomy involves the problem of atmospheric turbulence. In this application, the laser creates an object to be measured. It is not involved in the measurement itself.

The problem astronomers seek to address is atmospheric turbulence and its effect on Earth-bound observations. There is a tremendous ocean of air between every Earth-based telescope and the celestial objects it was built to observe, and like every ocean, Earth's atmosphere is continually in motion. Masses of air, each with its own temperature, density, and humidity swirl continuously overhead, distorting the images formed by the telescope. For centuries, the only solution available to astronomers was to build telescopes on high mountains, above as much of the atmosphere as possible. Indeed, all large research telescopes are now located on mountains. It is a solution that minimizes atmospheric distortions, but it does not eliminate them.

Today, there are two other ways for astronomers to obviate the distortions caused by Earth's atmosphere. The first involves placing the

Using a laser to generate an artificial guide star at the Keck II telescope. Adaptive optics has led to enormous improvements in the resolution of ground-based telescopes, but without laser guide stars, adaptive optics-equipped telescopes are limited to observing objects that happen to line up with naturally occurring guide stars. [U.S. Department of Energy]

observatory entirely above the atmosphere. This, for example, explains why the *Hubble Space Telescope* proved to be such a boon for astronomers. In comparison with other research telescopes, *Hubble's* size was modest—an important factor since the resolution of a telescope, its ability to distinguish detail, is limited by the size of the mirror used to collect and focus incoming light. Even at the time of its launch, there were Earth-bound telescopes much larger than *Hubble*. What made *Hubble* such a valuable astronomical instrument was that the views obtained with it were entirely free of any distortions caused by Earth's atmosphere.

The second solution to the problem of atmospheric distortion is, if anything, more technically challenging than putting a telescope in orbit. It is this second solution that depends essentially on lasers. The idea is based on a new concept of what a mirror can do. All early telescope mirrors were simple geometric surfaces. They were ground to very exact specifications, covered with a highly reflective coating, and then carefully positioned in the telescope, where they functioned as passive light collectors. New mirrors, by contrast, are dynamic surfaces. Rather than being composed of a single slab of extremely heavy glass, they are composed of many thin, carefully surfaced mirror components. Each component has a number of devices attached to its back called actuators. The actuators are capable of initiating many small changes in the shape of the mirror component each second. The technology has been used to create huge mirrors, many times larger than *Hubble's*, composed of many smaller component mirrors. When in use, the main mirror continually changes shape as the telescope itself responds to changes in Earth's atmosphere. Essentially, the mirror is rippling in a way that undoes the distortions in the images of celestial objects caused by atmospheric turbulence. This technology is called adaptive optics.

Creating a dynamic telescope mirror is an extraordinary technical challenge. The component mirrors must be made to extremely precise technical specifications, as must the actuators. A great deal of computational power is required to compute and recompute the correct shape of the mirror and to accomplish this in real time, because the effects of the atmosphere on the light that passes through it are continually changing. In many applications of adaptive optics, the data on which the computations are based come from measurements on a secondary object. The idea is to perform two sets of observations simultaneously. One set of observations concern the astronomical object of interest. These astronomical observations are the reason that the telescope was built. But in order that the observations succeed, the telescope mirror upon which they depend must be continually flexed and bent in certain very specific ways, many times each second, so that the distortions in the image caused by the atmosphere are undone. The data necessary to flex the mirror are gleaned from a secondary set of observations on the other astronomical object. This secondary object is often a star, but other celestial objects have been used as well. Because atmospheric distortions are local, that is, the distortions in one direction are different from those in another, the secondary, or reference, object on which the computations depend must be close to the primary object from the point of view of the telescope. This is still the best method of obtaining the information needed to use the adaptive optics hardware, but it suffers from a severe drawback: Oftentimes, there is no suitable reference object—also called a guide star—and astronomers are left with a choice. Do they restrict their choice of targets to those located near guide stars, or do they attempt to create their own artificial guide star? Artificial guide stars are created using a laser.

The most common technique for creating a laser guide star, or LGS, depends on the existence of sodium atoms in the upper atmosphere. Beginning at an altitude of about 56 miles (90 km) above Earth's surface, there is a layer of sodium atoms. The layer extends out for about 6.2 miles (10 km), and it is thought to be due to micro-meteorites burning up in the upper atmosphere. These atoms can be excited—in other words, their energy level can be elevated—by a laser emitting light at a wavelength of 589 nanometers (nm). As the energy level of the sodium atoms drop back to their *ground state*, they emit photons at a wavelength of 589 nm, and the result is a compact, softly glowing patch of sky. This is the LGS used to provide input to the adaptive optics software.

Creating a useful LGS has proved quite difficult. Sodium concentrations in the upper atmosphere vary from hour to hour and even minute to minute, and because the LGS is in the upper atmosphere, its optical properties are somewhat different from those of the star it seeks to emulate. Despite these difficulties, engineers and scientists around the world have devoted a great deal of time to creating these artificial stars. Several solutions have been proposed. Some have used CW lasers, others pulsed lasers of different designs. The reason for all this work is simple. Without LGSs, these enormous, expensive, sophisticated telescopes are limited to observing only those astronomical objects that happen to lie near suitable reference stars.

As of this writing the most successful solutions to the problem of producing an LGS involve what is called a dye laser. Dye lasers are different from the other types of lasers considered so far because the lasing medium is a liquid. A liquid containing the desired dye is put into a sealed tube. The dye is a fairly complex molecule and can absorb and emit light at a wide variety of wavelengths. Whereas an Nd:YAG laser, for example, will emit light at 1,064 nm, a dye laser can be created to emit a wide spectrum of electromagnetic radiation at visible wavelengths. The output of a dye laser will depend both on the wavelength(s) of the light used to *pump* the lasing medium and the composition of the dye. Depending on how the lasing medium is excited a dye laser can produce a rainbow of colors. This enables the designer to introduce devices at the output end of the lasing medium to select one or more wavelengths from which to create a laser beam. The selected wavelengths can be further processed with lenses, amplifiers, and other tools of the trade to produce the desired type and power of light. The Keck astronomical observatory in Hawaii, for example, has used a dye laser that is pumped by six Nd:YAG lasers to create their

LGS. The light, produced at a wavelength of 589 nm, is amplified to create a 17-watt beam that, when further focused and aimed skyward, creates an LGS in the upper reaches of Earth's atmosphere.

The lasers used to create the guide stars introduce problems of their own, and creating a useful one is still an active area of research. Some of the problems are difficult to avoid. The powers necessary to create an LGS can also pose a hazard to aircraft and even satellites to the extent that they can disrupt sensors on satellites and endanger the vision of pilots. In fact, the U.S. government has imposed restrictions on the use of lasers to create guide stars. These restrictions have sometimes required astronomers to interrupt their observations, shut off the laser, and wait while satellites pass overhead. Another difficulty with LGS involves the scattering of laser light. Ordinary telescopic observations can sometimes proceed even in the presence of thin, high-altitude cirrus clouds, but the ice in the clouds causes scattering of the laser beam before it has reached the sodium layer. The scattering causes light pollution, which hinders observations, and also prevents the formation of an effective guide star. Despite these difficulties, LGSs remain the best way to make full use of the current generation of telescopes outfitted with adaptive optics technology.

10

HOLOGRAPHY, ART, AND SCIENCE IN THREE DIMENSIONS

Holograms are a medium for storing three-dimensional information. They stand in the same relation to photography that sculpture stands in relation to oil painting. Holograms, though they are not nearly as common as photographs, have, nevertheless, become fairly commonplace. Small, extremely simple holograms can be found on many bank cards as a security measure. The magazine *National Geographic* has released a few issues that feature holograms on the front cover—the December 1988 issue is particularly well known—and the U.S. Postal Service has issued a holographic stamp. But holography will not soon replace photography as a visual medium. Holograms do not capture colors as well as traditional photography; they are often harder to view, and as a consequence, they may seem inferior to photographs, but they are not. Holograms record information that one cannot capture with traditional photography.

The science of holography was conceived in 1948 by Hungarian-born scientist Dennis Gabor (1900–79). He was searching for a way to improve the resolution of the electron microscope, and he discovered the principles of holography. Although he understood the theory of holography, and he published his results, his insights did

A photograph of a hologram of the discoverer of holography, Dennis Gabor (1900–79). Unfortunately, photographs of holograms are neither holograms nor very clear photographs. [Science Museum, London/Topham-HIP/The Image Works]

not immediately lead to the creation of any but the poorest quality holograms. Gabor's idea was ahead of its time, because in order to create a hologram one needs a light source that is coherent. In 1948 there were no coherent light sources. Holograms could not become a reality until the creation of the *laser*.

More on the Nature of Light

To understand how holograms work, it helps to look a little more deeply into the wave nature of light, especially the phenomenon of *interference*. Recall from chapter 1 that two waves can occupy the same space at the same time. When two waves overlap, their waveforms combine in a straightforward way to produce a new waveform. The new wave, called the resultant, is the sum of the component waves. Consider the two simple waves with identical *wavelengths* pictured in the diagram below. When the peaks of the component waves coincide in space, the peak of the resultant is the sum of the *amplitudes*. In particular, the amplitude of the resultant is greater than the amplitude of either component. But if the peak of one of the component waves coincides with the trough of the other, then cancellation occurs, and the amplitude of the resultant wave is less than the amplitude of the larger of the two component waves. (In fact, in this special case the two waves completely cancel each other and the amplitude is zero.) This is an example of the phenomenon of interference.

In order to describe the way that two simple waves interfere with each other, it is not enough, therefore, to know only the amplitude and wavelength of the waves. It is also necessary to be able to specify the position of the peaks. If the peaks of the component waves coincide as in diagram (a), the two waves are said to be in *phase*. If one wave is shifted somewhat relative to the other as in diagram (b), then the two waves are out of phase. But notice that if one wave is shifted sufficiently far to the right or left, the two waves will be back in phase again. Even with two simple and otherwise identical waveforms, it is possible to get

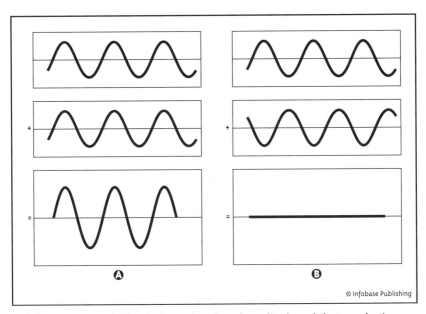

© Infobase Publishing

In (a) two waves with identical wavelength and amplitude and that are also in phase combine to form a resultant wave whose amplitude is double that of either component wave. In (b) the same waves are entirely out of phase, and so the resultant has zero amplitude.

a variety of different resultant waves simply by shifting the phase of one wave relative to the other.

Using this terminology, it is now possible to describe in a very general way how holograms differ from photographs: Color photographs capture information about the frequency and amplitude of the light that forms the image. When light strikes an object, some of the light is absorbed and some reflected. As a general rule, each material reflects certain wavelengths of light better than others, and in the process of taking a photograph some of this reflected light enters the lens of the camera. Remember that a simple wave has three properties: wavelength, amplitude, and phase. (It is sufficient to restrict the discussion to simple waves, because more complex waves can always be represented as the resultant, or sum, of a collection of simple waves.) Ordinary cameras, film or digital, record the color and intensity of the light that enters the camera. Or to put it another way, ordinary cameras record information about the light's wavelength (color) and amplitude (intensity). Photographs record no information about the phase of the incident light.

Holograms, by contrast, do record information about the phase of the incident light. They also record information about the intensity of the light, and if the hologram is a color hologram, it will also contain information about the wavelength of the incident light. (As with ordinary photographs, holograms may or may not record color. The details of color holography will not be addressed here.) It is this additional property of a hologram, its ability to record the phase of the light reflected off the subject that distinguishes the hologram from the photograph. It is an extremely important distinction, and it is the reason that holograms have many surprising properties that photographs do not, indeed cannot, have.

One more note: The model of a light wave as a sinusoidal waveform is useful for developing the vocabulary and concepts associated with waves, but in three-dimensional space—and it is the three-dimensional nature of the subject that holograms are designed to record—it is often more convenient to imagine light as consisting of a series of wave fronts, surfaces that propagate through space, rather than a sinusoidal curve that propagates along a line. The intensity of the passing wave fronts corresponds to the amplitudes of the simple sinusoidal curves considered in the previous paragraphs. The wave fronts that emanate from most sources spread out as they travel through space, but the wave fronts emitted by lasers remain compact and coherent over long distances. It is this property of lasers, their ability to emit well defined wave fronts that makes holograms possible.

Creating a Hologram

First, a note about terminology: The medium on which a hologram is recorded will be described as "film," in part, because many applications of holography involve film. (The type of film used in holography is capable of capturing extremely fine detail; its performance far exceeds that of the digital cameras and the types of photographic films with which most of us are familiar.) Although not every hologram is stored on film, there is no convenient term that includes all holographic storage media, and enumerating each type of storage medium each time

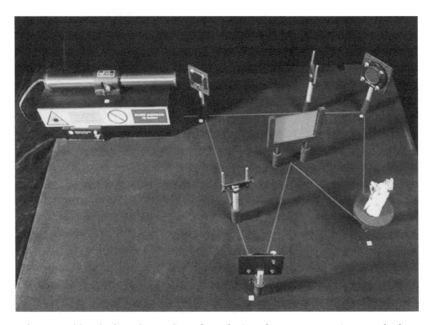

Hologram table. The laser beam shows how the interference pattern is created: The beam emanates from the laser on the left and passes through the beam splitter. The reference beam emerges from the beam splitter and is directed toward the right, and the object beam continues along a straight path. Next, each passes through a lens and is reflected off a mirror. The reference beam is directed toward the plate, while the object beam is directed toward the object on the round pedestal, which reflects some of the light toward the plate, where an interference pattern is generated. [SSPL/The Image Works]

the discussion requires a reference to such media is awkward. The word *film* in this context is, then, a generic term for any holographic storage media.

How do holographers record information on the phase of the incident light? The film that is used for holography could just as easily be used to record a photograph, and photographs contain no information at all about the phase of the light waves. The difference between a photograph and a hologram lies in the image that appears on the film used to create a hologram. In contrast to a photo, which forms an image of the subject, the hologram forms an interference pattern. In effect, the subject of the hologram is an interference pattern. That interference pattern is later used to create an image of the original object, but if one examines the image on the film, one finds only a spaghetti-like collection of closely packed lines and curves, a record of the interference pattern that the holographer created.

The first step in creating a hologram is to obtain the equipment. There is surprisingly little equipment required. First, the holographer must obtain a laser that produces the purest monochromatic (single-wavelength) light and the most coherent beam available. In theory every laser produces monochromatic light—or in the case of a dye laser, for example, several pure wavelengths simultaneously from which one wavelength can be chosen—but in practice there are always some unwanted, low-amplitude wavelengths emitted along with "the" laser light. The situation is analogous to a sound recording. A CD produces much less hiss than an LP, but even with a CD there are the occasional noises resulting from scratches, stray voltages, and so on.

The same sort of statement can be made about the coherency of laser light. Laser light is highly coherent, but over a long enough distance—the length of which depends on the quality of the laser—the beam eventually loses its coherency. The longer the light emitted by the laser retains its coherency, the better suited that laser is to the process of holography. The lesson is this: A laser is always a far better source of monochromatic, coherent light than an incandescent bulb, but there is always some difference between theory and practice. Some lasers produce better, or more monochromatic light, than others.

Next, one needs a device called a beam splitter. This is a simple optical device into which one shines the laser. The beam splitter divides the laser beam into two component beams that emerge in different directions. They have names: One is called the reference beam, and the other is called the image or object beam. It is the interaction of these two beams on the film that creates the interference pattern.

The reference beam is directed by one or more mirrors—it depends on the geometry of the setup—toward the film. As it makes its way toward the film, the reference beam will also generally pass through one or more lenses. This is done so that the reference beam will expand and illuminate the entire film. Otherwise, the reference beam is unaltered. In particular, there is no concept of focusing the light on the film as is done in photography. The reference beam consists of an unadulterated set of planar wave fronts, which are, in effect, a record of the light that first emanated from the laser.

The other beam that emerges from the beam splitter, the object beam, is used to illuminate the object that is to appear in the hologram. The object beam is often redirected one or more times with mirrors, and it, too, passes through a lens in order to broaden the beam sufficiently to illuminate the object. It is also helpful to imagine the object beam as a series of planar wave fronts—at least until the object beam impinges on the object itself. Notice that in the diagram on page 130, the object is an apple. If one imagines a planar wave front impinging on the apple, it is not difficult to see that because the surface of the apple is curved, different parts of the wave front will reach the apple at different times. As a consequence, they are reflected by the apple at different times and in different directions. The resulting reflection is a highly distorted version of the original planar wave front. That part of the wave front that impinged on the most forward part of the apple is reflected first. Those parts of the planar front that strike the parts of the apple that are farther back will be reflected later. It is a simplification, but a helpful one, to imagine that the reflected front carries a three-dimensional image of the apple on it. A more accurate, but more complex, way of imagining what is happening is to picture each point of the apple reflecting light outward in an ever expanding front, much the way a circular water wave expands out across the surface of a quiet pond at the drop of a pebble. Some of this reflected light is cast across the film, which is also illuminated with the reference wave. Taken together, these two light sources, the reference beam and the object beam, form an interference pattern on the film, and, in fact, the goal of this entire process is to obtain a permanent record of this interference pattern.

Obtaining a usable interference pattern is not easy. The interference pattern is extremely delicate in the sense that if any of the holographic equipment is vibrated, the interference pattern is smeared, and the hologram is ruined. The amount of motion needed to ruin a hologram is measured in fractions of a wavelength of the reference

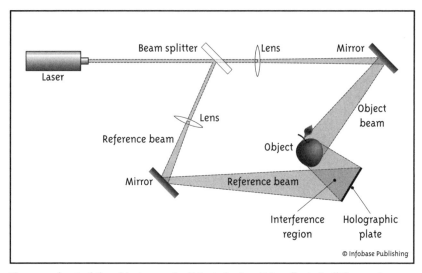

The wave front of the object wave is distorted when it is reflected off the apple. The resultant wave pattern formed on the holographic plate by the distorted object wave and the undistorted reference wave can be used to create a three-dimensional image of the apple.

beam, an unimaginably small amount of movement. For this reason, holographers must give a great deal of thought to the table used to support their equipment. Tables weighing several tons are common as are various clever techniques to dampen any remaining vibrations.

Once the holographer completes the exposure, the film is developed. What remains bears the same relation to the light that shone on the film that a plaster cast has to a sculpture around which it was formed. It was, for example, once common practice to make casts of famous sculptures with the goal of making replicas. These casts are the mechanical analogues of holograms. There are casts of many Greek works as well as the statues of Michelangelo. The method involved forming a plaster cast around the statue and then removing it. What was retained was the three-dimensional structure of the object. The cast was then pieced together and used to create duplicates. In the same way, the interference pattern recorded on the film is a sort of cast of the light that impinged upon it.

One way of recovering the desired image from the interference pattern is to place the developed film in front of the reference beam. As the light passes through the film, the interference pattern dampens the amplitude of the light and redirects the passing wave front to create the same wave front that was reflected off the original object. In this sense, the film can be pictured as an extremely complex lens that alters the planar wave front as it passes through to produce a new wave front with many of the properties of the object beam after it reflected off the object. The resulting hologram is a three-dimensional object. One can, for example, look at it from the left and see the left side of the subject, or if one looks at the hologram from the right, the right side becomes visible, but the left side of the subject is no longer visible. When the holographic image is obtained by shining the reference wave back through the film, one obtains what is called a transmission hologram.

Another type of hologram, called a reflection hologram, does not require a coherent light source to shine through it from the back. The light necessary to make these holographic images appear comes from the observer's side of the hologram. These images are created in such a way that when incident light composed of a variety of wavelengths is shone upon the hologram, various wavelengths are absorbed as they pass into the hologram. What emerges, or is reflected back toward the observer, is that wavelength of light chosen to make the hologram

The easiest place to find a hologram is on a credit card, where it is used as a security device. Unfortunately, these are usually too simple to be of much interest. To see how much information can be conveyed via a hologram, a holography exhibit at a museum is still the best place to go. [Pegasus/Visuals Unlimited]

appear. These holograms are more common because they can be viewed without the hardware needed to see a transmission hologram. They are also somewhat more problematic since they depend crucially on ambient lighting and the willingness of the observer to tilt and squint at the hologram until it appears. There is a corresponding loss of control by the hologram creator over the quality of the final image.

Properties of Holograms

One of the most remarked upon properties of holograms concerns what one can see if a hologram is cut into pieces. The reason that this attracts so much attention is that it contrasts so sharply with what happens when a photograph is cut in half. Suppose, for example, that a photograph of a woman's face is cut in half and the lower half is thrown away. In this case, the observer loses a great deal of information. Was the woman smiling? Was she wearing lipstick? Did she have a beard? These questions are impossible to answer without looking at the missing half of the photograph. By contrast, if one makes a hologram of the same woman's face, and the hologram is cut in half and the lower half is thrown away, all of this information is preserved in the upper half of the hologram. The lower half of the woman's face remains visible in the upper half of the hologram, and so all of the questions previously posed can be answered. What is lost when the lower half of the hologram is thrown away?

Imagine that a person is seated behind a window. One can look into the window from a variety of angles, and from each angle that person is visible. Of course, if one views the person from the right side, one cannot see the left side of the individual's face. Nevertheless, most people would still assert that they can see the individual because from their perspective the "entire" individual is visible. The perspective that one has depends upon that part of the window from which the individual is viewed, but each perspective provides the observer with a view of the individual.

Now suppose that one places paper over the bottom half of the window—the analogue of cutting a hologram in half and throwing away the bottom half—then the number of ways one has of seeing the person is similarly restricted. Blocking out the lower half of the window in no way interferes with any of the views one can obtain by looking through the upper half of the window. The person is just as visible from any of these perspectives as previously. All that has been eliminated are the views that one would obtain by looking through the bottom half of the window. A similar situation arises when a hologram is cut in half. The remaining half provides all the perspectives that it did previously. In this sense, holograms are more robust than photographs. The reason that holograms have this peculiar property is that each hologram is a three-dimensional object, a sort of light sculpture, and each section of the hologram provides its own view of the object independently of the existence of other parts of the hologram.

Another property of holograms that makes them different from photographs involves the light used to illuminate the hologram. In the case of a transmission hologram, this is done with a laser, the wavelength of which may or may not equal that of the reference beam. One can, for example, create the hologram with red light and display the image with blue light. The hologram will bend red light more than blue, however, with the result that the blue image will appear smaller than the red image. No information is lost if the shorter wavelength is employed; the hologram looks as good in blue as it did in red, but because the size of the image depends on the wavelength of the light used to reconstruct it, difficulties arise when one tries to illuminate the hologram with incandescent light. Multiple images are formed as each of the component wavelengths is brought to a focus in a slightly different place. The result is a smeared image.

Scientists have worked hard to address the problems associated with holograms, and today there are techniques for creating holograms that can be displayed with ordinary incandescent light as well as for making color holograms. The techniques are only partially successful, however. Green-faced portraits and blurred, ghostly images of solid unghostly objects are still characteristic of many holograms. Despite these drawbacks, holography continues to attract the attention of artists and scientists alike. For many artists, the possibility of making a three-dimensional sculpture out of light remains an attractive possibility. For scientists, holograms promise other possibilities: Three-dimensional data displays, improved analysis of fluid flow, a security medium, and improved microscopy are four contemporary applications.

Still another use of holograms, one which is both technologically important and uses the ideas developed in this and preceding chapters, is in the area of optical data storage. In the early 1960s, scientists calculated that by employing holograms as a kind of data storage device, one could achieve a storage capacity in the neighborhood of one bit per cubic wavelength. For lasers operating in the visible part of the spectrum, one wavelength is a small distance, indeed. Cubing the

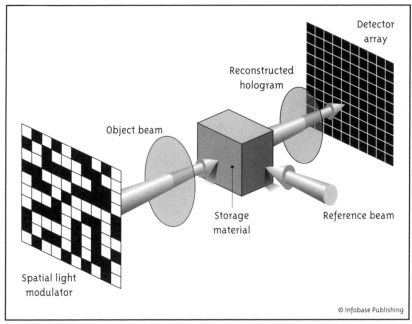

A schematic of a holographic data storage system. By changing the angle of the reference beam, many holographic images can be stored within the same volume of storage material without one image interfering with another.

wavelength makes for an extremely small volume. The result is that, at least in theory, holograms could be used to store data at a density of roughly one terabyte per cubic centimeter. (This is written as 1 TB/cm^3 or to put it another way: 1,024 gigabytes of data can be stored in one cubic centimeter of storage medium.) Such an astonishingly high theoretical storage capacity sparked a great deal of research into the use of holograms for data storage, but the work was eventually abandoned because the technical challenges could not be overcome at the time. Scientists needed to find a way to encode the data in holographic form, to read the resulting hologram, and to develop a "thick" medium in which to store the holograms. In the 1990s, engineers and scientists began to solve each of these three problems, and holographic data storage is again a very active area of research.

The accompanying diagram shows one method by which holograms can be used to store data. As with any hologram, two laser beams, an object beam and a reference beam, are required. The object beam shines through a device called a spatial light modulator. It consists of a large number of optical gates, or pixels, that can be independently opened and closed. The pattern of open and closed gates represents the information to be stored. When the object beam is directed at the modulator, the pattern modulates the object beam, which then combines with the reference beam inside the storage medium to create the hologram. (Notice that the pattern stored in the hologram is flat or two-dimensional.) To recover the data, one shines the reference beam into the storage medium, and the original pattern of dark and light spots appears on a light-sensitive device that "recaptures" the data for processing.

Notice, first, that data is recorded and retrieved in entire pages rather than bit by bit. There is, then, the possibility of extremely high data transfer rates. But what makes this method especially powerful is the way the reference beam interacts with the storage medium. In order to recover the hologram, the reference beam must be directed into the storage medium at the same angle that was used to store the hologram. In particular, if the angle at which the beam is shown differs from the original, the hologram cannot be displayed. Far from being a disadvantage, this dependence of the hologram on the angle of the reference beam is a tremendous advantage. By changing the angle at which the reference beam is directed, one can store thousands of holograms in the same place inside the storage medium. Properly done, the holograms do not interfere with one another, and only one can be recovered at a time. Current technology has enabled engineers to store approximately 10,000 holograms in the same 1 cm^3 region, and because it is stored and read in pages rather than bit by bit, they can be stored and recovered very quickly.

Just as the lasers that create them, holograms, too, hold great promise. The difference is that lasers found almost immediate application. The technical problems associated with holograms were, apparently, more formidable, and the practical use of holograms has always seemed just slightly beyond reach since their discovery half a century ago. Some of these problems are being solved today, however, and holograms may soon be as ubiquitous as lasers.

11

ILLUMINATING THE INVISIBLE

P revious chapters have described the use of *lasers* in medicine, industry, measurement, and the transmission and storage of information, but lasers can also be used to simply illuminate objects and materials in ways that were previously impossible. This aspect of lasers has also proved to be extremely useful. Recall from chapter 1 that at its most basic level light exhibits two properties: It is energy in motion, and it is a medium by which information is conveyed. This second property, light as information, is more apparent when light is deliberately modulated so that information can be read by the receiver. Techniques for modulating light in order that it convey information were discussed, for example, in chapters 7, 8, and 10. But light *always* conveys information of some type. Light from distant galaxies, properly analyzed, contains information about the chemical composition of the component stars as well as the galaxy's distance from our own. At a more immediate level, light from across the room contains information about the shape of the room as well as the furniture and people contained therein. In neither case was information deliberately encoded on the light beams that bridged the gap separating the exterior world from the mind of the observer, but the information was there nonetheless. To obtain that

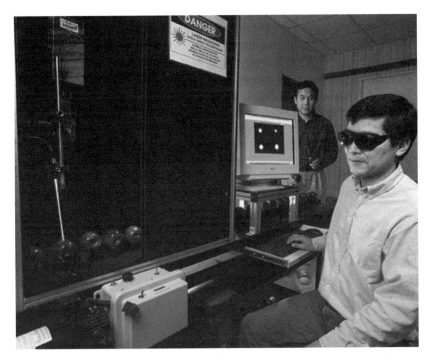

Spectroscopy is now a highly developed science. Spectrometers come in a variety of designs and have found application in many different fields. In this photo, a prototype laser-based spectrometer called a multispectral imaging system is used to measure the firmness and sugar content of apples. [Stephan Ausmus and U.S. Department of Agriculture]

information, one need only know how to interpret the light waves on which it was conveyed.

Because light is usually so rich in information—just consider how much they have learned from looking at pictures of places people have never visited—it should not be surprising that some types of light, or more precisely some types of electromagnetic energy, should be more revealing than others. Laser light is a new type of light, and since its discovery engineers and scientists have expended a great deal of effort learning to analyze the laser light reflected by target materials and objects. They are still learning to do just that. In particular, they have become adept at shining lasers at unknown objects and unknown materials and interpreting the reflected rays of the laser so as to reveal important and previously unknown facts.

Optical Microscopes and Lasers

An optical microscope enables the user to view objects when they are illuminated with light, as opposed to other forms of electromagnetic radiation. Optical microscopes existed long before lasers were created, and they remain an important part of the technology that one uses to view the very small. As with every technology, optical microscopes have certain limitations. In particular, they cannot be used to view objects below a certain size. The quality of the lenses affects the sharpness of the view, but there is another more fundamental restriction: the *wavelength* of the light used to make the observation. When features become too small compared to the wavelength of the light used to observe them, those features cannot be resolved. This is called the diffractive limit. The diffractive limit is about one-half wavelength. Violet, which of all the colors has the shortest wavelength, has a wavelength of 400 nanometer (nm). To observe features on an object smaller than 200 nm across, one needs to "look" using much shorter wavelengths. Electron microscopes, for example, are designed to use electrons with extremely short wavelengths. Their resolving power—their ability to distinguish detail—is much better than that of the best optical microscopes, but these instruments are expensive, and the preparation of the specimen is time consuming. Electron microscopes are important tools, but they are poorly suited to certain applications.

An interesting invention, patented in 2004 by a British company called Nanosight, uses a laser, an optical microscope, a computer, and some clever physics to determine the size of particles that are as small as 15 nm across. This is much smaller than the wavelength of any type of (visible) light. To appreciate how small 15 nm is, consider a 15-nm sphere and a billiard ball side by side. (A billiard ball is 2.25 inches [5.71 cm] in diameter.) Now suppose that both objects were expanded the same amount so that the 15-nm sphere became the size of the billiard ball. Under these conditions the billiard ball would expand to a sphere more than 180 miles (300 km) across. Objects 15 nm or even 150 nm across are well beyond the diffractive limit for an optical microscope, but Nanosight's device, called the Halo LM10, can measure the size of these nanoparticles, which allows the investigator to narrow the possibilities of what the particles in question might be. The system is robust in that specimens do not need a lot of preparation prior to observation, and the system can be used outside the lab.

The first step involves placing the sample in water or other fluid and then illuminating the suspension with a laser—in this case, a 20-milliwatt laser (one milliwatt, abbreviated one mW, equals one-thousandth of a watt). The laser emits red light at a wavelength of 650 nm. At 650 nm, the wavelength of the light used is simply too long to enable the investigator to "see" the particles in the sense that one can observe any distinguishing surface features. Instead, one observes bright spots of light bouncing around on the computer screen. The situation is analogous to observing a swarm of tiny insects under a streetlight. The insects are often so tiny that from a distance one cannot distinguish any detail at all. Their color, wing structure, body structure, and so on are all undetermined. They appear to be undifferentiated dots. Nevertheless, by observing how the swarm moves, one can often correctly deduce the species of insect that one is (not) seeing. Analogously, the laser provides an intense beam of light, the characteristics of which are simple and completely understood, that illuminates the particles. In the light of the laser, one sees bright red dots swarming about one's field of view with some moving faster than others. In fact, some of the video footage of the laser-illuminated nanoparticles shows them moving about in a way that is strongly reminiscent of a swarm of small insects. The particles are being jostled about the fluid in a phenomenon called Brownian motion.

Brownian motion was first observed by Scottish botanist Robert Brown (1773–1858). Brown noticed that pollen suspended in solution experienced small, rapid and apparently random motions. Although others had noticed the effect before him, Brown was the first to study the phenomenon. During the intervening years, Brownian motion has been studied extensively by mathematicians and physicists. Today, it is known that the pressure a fluid exerts on a body is the result of numerous random collisions between the body and the molecules (or atoms) of which the fluid is composed. For large bodies, differences in the force or number of collisions averages out over the body's surface, with the result that pressure seems uniformly distributed over its surface, but the situation is different for small bodies. When a body suspended in a fluid is small enough, there is not sufficient surface area on the body to permit the random collisions that continually occur to "average out." In such cases, significant, though fleeting, differences in pressure exerted by the molecules along the surface of the particle arise, and as a result the particle undergoes random motion.

Brown and other early scientists searched for a causative agent, something that would enable them to predict the motion of the particles. In one famous experiment, a particle-filled fluid was left sealed in a container for a year, after which time the observations were repeated. The outcome of the experiment was unchanged. Further observations revealed that particle size and fluid temperature and viscosity—a measure of the fluid's stickiness—are prime factors in determining the motion of the particles. Consequently, if one knows the particle size, one can predict the particle's motion, and conversely, if one can observe the particle's motion, one can, in theory, estimate the particle's size. The latter remark is the observation on which the Halo ML10 is based. If, for example, one suspends the particles in water, where the viscosity and other characteristic properties are known, one can compute what is called the hydrodynamic radius of each illuminated particle by measuring the motion of the particle and the temperature of the water. Keep in mind that one does not see the particle. Because of its small size, one cannot see the particle, using an optical microscope. One sees only a bright undifferentiated dot. Nevertheless, the motion of the particles yields a measure of particle size.

The computed hydrodynamic radius of particles can be combined with observations of the way that the particles present in the fluid scatter light from the laser to produce a fairly precise profile of the sizes of particles present in the fluid. Such profiles are important. Repeated measurements establish a statistical profile of normal particulate matter in the sampled medium. With this information, researchers are able to determine when new types of particulates are introduced, and all of this can be done in real time. The key is insightful physics, good software, and the right light.

Spectrometers

Spectroscopy is a branch of science founded on the observation that light emitted by an object, a star, for example, or reflected by an object, a planet, for example, carries with it information about the chemical composition of the object itself. It may sound as if spectroscopy is a very narrow discipline, but it is not. With respect to astronomy, it could not be more important. Without spectroscopy, virtually the entire universe is too far away to analyze chemically. Only electromagnetic energy bridges the tremendous distances that separate celestial objects from one another. But with spectroscopy the chemical composition of distant planets, stars, and galaxies is now known with certainty. This is an important scientific advance.

Today, applications of spectroscopy are everywhere. In addition to astronomy, it is now used to analyze everything from potentially hazardous substances to the sugar content of apples. Various techniques have evolved to meet the demands of specialists in a wide variety of scientific disciplines, and the technology continues to evolve as engineers and scientists search for faster, more accurate, and cheaper ways to learn about the world around us. Lasers are a vital part of this technology.

One common laser-based technique is called Raman spectroscopy. The device itself is called a *Raman spectrometer*. The name honors the Indian physicist Chandrasekhara Venkata Raman (1888–1970), who discovered that when light impinges on a transparent material some of the light that emerges is of a different wavelength than the source. This change in wavelength is caused by energy exchange between the sample and light used to illuminate it. This observation has had a profound impact on many aspects of science and is the concept on which the Raman spectrometer is based.

Raman spectrometer. This spectrometer is used to study the chemical and physical changes that occur in ceramic materials as they undergo friction. [Pacific Northwest National Laboratory]

To appreciate the ideas behind the Raman spectrometer, think of the sample as a kind of black box. In other words, the observer knows the input to the box, the output from the box, but initially nothing at all about what happens in between. One deduces the properties of the box by observing differences between the input and the output. With these ideas in mind, the Raman spectrometer can be modeled as an instrument with two parts, a laser (the input) and a detector, which measures the output. The laser is important because it is the form of light over which one can exercise the most control. In particular, the wavelength is known with certainty. Furthermore, laser light is very intense, an important consideration because most of the light that is scattered by the sample must be discarded.

The device works in the following way: First, the laser illuminates part of the sample. The coherent, single-wavelength light that was emitted by the laser is scattered everywhere. Some of this light illuminates the sensor on the detector. This light is the output of the process. It is almost identical with the input light, because the phenomenon that

Raman discovered is subtle. To measure it in terms of *photons*, only one out of every 10 million (or more) photons that is picked up by the detector has a wavelength that is different from those emitted by the laser. These new wavelengths are present because of interactions between the sample and the laser light. The *spectrum* of these new wavelengths reveals information about the structure and composition of the sample.

It is not surprising that such a subtle effect requires considerable processing, and also emphasizes how central a laser is to the process. The detector filters out the unaltered light, which, because it was emitted by the laser, can be identified with a great deal of precision. The light that remains is passed through a device to reveal the component wavelengths in the same sort of way that a rainbow reveals the visible wavelengths of which sunlight is composed.

Finally, the spectrum of the altered light is analyzed. Because different chemical compounds interact with the light in different and well-known ways, the spectrum revealed by the detector indicates the chemical composition of the sample in question. Raman spectrometers are an important tool in spectroscopy, but as with every technology, Raman spectrometers also have their shortcomings.

Alternatives to the Raman spectrometer exist, in part because this type of spectrometer is expensive. Lasers are always described as sources of "pure" light, but in practice every laser beam contains a little "noise"—wavelengths other than the one intended. But the phenomenon on which the spectrometer is based is a very delicate one. In order to be successful, the quality of the light emitted by the laser must be tightly controlled, otherwise the Raman effect is obscured by laser noise. The better controlled the laser light is, the more expensive the instrument becomes. Fortunately, another, more robust method is also in use. It is not the most accurate method available, but it works in real time with virtually no sample preparation at a more affordable price. The device is called a laser-induced breakdown spectrometer (LIBS).

The idea behind LIBS is to direct a high-power laser on a sample to create *plasma*, a gaslike substance that conducts electricity and responds to magnetic fields. The plasma created by an LIBS system is sometimes called a laser spark. As the name implies, the laser spark occurs very quickly, and the temperatures involved are extreme, thousands or even millions of degrees Celsius. At these energy levels, electrons are briefly stripped from the atoms with which they were associated and, like the ions they leave behind, move freely throughout the plasma.

One kind of laser that is often used to create the spark upon which LIBS depends is a Nd:YAG, *Q-switched* laser. While the laser may generate only a few tens of millijoules per pulse, the pulses are very short—on the order of a few nanoseconds—and so the laser is extremely powerful. (Recall from chapter 2 that laser power is a measure of how much energy is emitted per unit time. One can increase laser power by increasing the energy emitted over a given time interval or by decreasing the amount of time needed to emit a given amount of energy or both.) To further increase the beam's intensity, it is usually directed through one or more lenses. The result is a laser beam that may well emit power that is measured in megawatts per unit area, but only because the area on which it is concentrated is so small. The goal of this is to create a laser powerful enough to produce the laser spark.

As indicated in the preceding paragraphs, the heating process is extremely brief—only a few nanoseconds—and the amount of plasma created is minute. It is no exaggeration to say that as soon as the laser is off, the glowing plasma begins to cool rapidly. Keep in mind that the amount of hot material is small, and it is surrounded by a comparatively cool environment with the capacity to absorb the heat of the spark without a significant increase in the ambient temperature. As the plasma cools, electrons and ions begin to recombine to form neutral atoms, and the excited atoms begin to return to their ground state.

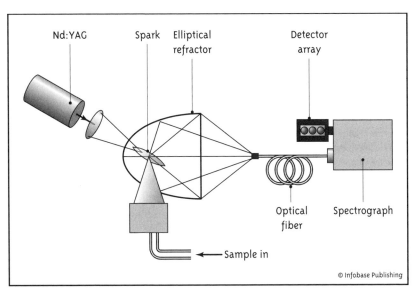

© Infobase Publishing

Schematic of a laser-induced breakdown spectrometer (LIBS). The sample meets the laser at the location labeled spark, which is positioned at one focus of the ellipsoid. The resulting light waves are reflected by the ellipsoidal mirror toward the other focus, where they are picked up by fiber-optic filament and carried to a spectrograph, a device used to analyze the resulting waveform.

During the cooling process, photons are spontaneously emitted, and it is these photons, whose frequencies (energies) depend upon the chemical composition of the sample, that provide the input for the detector. Because this is a very high energy process, energy is released along a very broad band in the electromagnetic spectrum. As a consequence, the input to the detector is information-rich; there is a lot to analyze.

An ellipsoidal mirror is sometimes employed to collect the light of the spark and bring it to a focus. (The brighter the image, the more there is to analyze.) To accomplish this, the spark is generated at one focus of the ellipsoid. Recall from chapter 3 that those light waves generated at one focus of the ellipsoid will radiate outward and—providing they strike the mirror—will be directed by the mirror toward the other focus of the ellipsoid. Optical fibers placed at the second focus collect the light and direct it toward the detector, where the signal is decomposed into its component wavelengths. Because the plasma created by the laser is quickly cooling and the energy state of the atoms is dropping as they emit photons on their path back to their ground state, the nature of the spectrum is continually changing. Numerous measurements are made at the detector to capture as much of the changing nature of the light as possible. All of this information is stored and analyzed to produce a series of graphs that can be used to identify the chemical components of the sample. The result is a fairly refined analysis of the sample in question.

The process is not delicate. In contrast to Raman spectroscopy, LIBS does not require a finely tuned laser, nor does it require extensive sample preparation. In a sense, it is a point-and-shoot technique. This is its advantage: It is simple and robust. While there are laser-based spectrometers of other designs that can reliably identify materials present in concentrations of parts per trillion, LIBS can yield real-time analyses that identify materials present in concentrations of parts per million—sometimes less—and it can accomplish this cheaply and with reasonable accuracy. LIBS is now used in situations in which it is necessary to frequently monitor air and water quality, for example.

Lasers, once widely believed to be impossible to construct, can now be found everywhere. They are, in a certain sense, a new type of machine, the first of a class of machines whose operating principles are derived from discoveries in the field of quantum mechanics, a field of knowledge that did not exist until the first half of the 20th century. This book has enumerated only some of the ways that lasers are used. There are far too many different applications to describe in any one book, and the field continues to evolve. New applications for this remarkable machine continue to be discovered on a regular basis. Lasers have made an enormous difference to our lives and are rightly classified as one of the most important inventions of the 20th century.

PREFIXES

Prefixes indicating small units:

Milli-	One thousandth	0.001
Micro-	One millionth	0.000001
Nano-	One billionth	0.000000001
Pico-	One trillionth	0.000000000001
Femto-	One quadrillionth	0.000000000000001

Prefixes indicating large units:

Mega-	One million	1,000,000
Giga-	One billion	1,000,000,000
Tera-	One trillion	1,000,000,000,000

GLOSSARY

amplitude   With respect to a wave, one-half the distance from peak to trough.

beam splitter   A device used to split one laser beam into two or more beams.

coherence   Two or more waves whose phase relationship does not change over time.

continuous wave (CW) laser   A laser that emits a steady, uninterrupted beam for an indefinite time period.

duty cycle   For a laser that emits pulses of light regularly, the duty cycle is the ratio of the duration of time that the laser emits light to the total time elapsed from the beginning of one pulse to the beginning of the next.

efficiency   For a laser, the ratio of the energy of the emitted wave to the energy supplied by the power source.

electromagnetic wave   Wave consisting of periodic variations of electric and magnetic energy and including radio, micro-, infrared, visible light, ultraviolet, X-ray, and gamma-ray waves.

energy   The capacity to do work.

energy level   Any one of a set of discrete states of constant energy assumed by an atom or molecule.

frequency   The number of waves to pass a given point per unit time.

ground state   The lowest energy level of an atom or molecule.

hologram   A three-dimensional image created from the interference pattern formed by a reference beam and an object beam.

index of refraction   The ratio of the speed of light in a vacuum to the speed of light in another medium.

interference   The mutual effect of the intermingling of two wave fronts.

joule Unit of work or energy.

laser Acronym for "light amplification by stimulated emission of radiation," a device that through the process of stimulated emission produces an intense, coherent, monochromatic light.

laser induced breakdown spectroscopy (LIBS) A device used to determine the composition of a material from emissions given off by the plasma formed by radiating a sample of the material.

lidar Acronym for "light detection and ranging," a device similar to radar but which emits light waves.

maser Acronym for "microwave amplification by stimulated emission of radiation," a device similar in concept to a laser but which produces energy in the microwave portion of the spectrum.

metastable state An energy level that shows relative stability at a state higher than the ground state.

modulate To vary the amplitude, frequency, or phase of a carrier wave.

monochromatic light A light source consisting of waves of identical wavelength.

oscillate To move back and forth between locations.

patent A document conferred on an inventor granting exclusive rights to make, sell, or license an invention.

phase The position with respect to some reference point of a simple wave form.

photocoagulation To coagulate tissue using a laser.

photon One quantum of electromagnetic radiation.

plasma Gaslike substance that conducts electricity and responds to magnetic fields.

power The rate of working per unit time.

pulse-position modulation (PPM) A particular scheme for modulating a wave to carry information.

pump To raise the energy level of a lasing medium with the goal of creating a population inversion.

Q-switch Any of a class of devices designed to control the resonant properties of the laser cavity.

quantum A very small discrete parcel of energy.

radiation The process of emitting energy in the form of waves or particles.

Raman spectrometer A device for producing and investigating spectra with the goal of determining the composition of an object.

resonate Enhancing or amplifying a signal via the oscillation of an initially weak impulse.

spectrometer Any of a class of devices used to produce and analyze spectra.

spectroscopy   That discipline of science concerned with the production and analysis of spectra.

spectrum   Some subset of the continuum of electromagnetic waves arranged according to wavelength.

spontaneous emission   The emission of a photon by an atom or molecule as it makes the transition to a state of lower energy.

stimulated emission   The phenomenon that occurs when an atom or molecule in a state of higher energy is passed by a photon of a certain wavelength and stimulated to emit a second photon.

Universal Product Code (UPC)   The first-bar code labeling system to come into general use.

watt   Unit of power (1 watt = 1 joule per second).

wavelength   The distance between successive peaks or troughs of a wave.

work   Force applied over a distance, a quantity usually measured in joules.

FURTHER READING

Berner, Jeff. *The Holography Book.* New York: Avon Books, 1980. This is a story of how holography has been used to create art works. Unfortunately, none of the pictures are holographic, but there is a lot of information here.

Blake, Ives. "Custom Made Apparel and Individualized Service at Land's End." *Communications of the Association for Information Systems.* 11, article 3, January 2003. Available online. URL: http://cais.isworld.org/articles/11-3/article.pdf. This is a case study of how the partial implementation of mass customization has affected the fortunes of one of America's big clothing retailers. It is not technical. In fact, lasers are barely mentioned. It is interesting, nevertheless, because it shows how these ideas can be implemented in practice.

Boraiko, Allen A. "The Laser, A Splendid Light for Man's Use." *National Geographic,* March 1984, pp. 335–377. The text is old, but the photographs are still second to none.

Freitas, Frank de, Alan Rhody, and Stephen W. Michael. *Shoebox Holography: A Step-by-step Guide to Making Holograms Using Inexpensive Semiconductor Lasers.* Berkeley, Calif.: Ross Books, 2000. There is no better way to learn than by doing.

Hecht, Jeff. *City of Light: The Story of Fiber Optics.* New York: Simon & Schuster, 2000. Without fiber optics, lasers would be far less useful; without lasers there would be less demand for fiber optics. This is the story of a vital enabling technology.

———. *The Laser Guidebook, Second Edition.* New York: McGraw-Hill, 1992. This book describes the nuts and bolts of lasers. It is a worthwhile reference.

———. *Laser Pioneers.* Boston: Academic Press, 1992. Interviews with a number of people who have been intimately involved in the development of laser technology and its uses.

———, and Dick Teresi. *Laser: Light of a Million Uses.* Mineola, N.Y.: Dover Publications, 1998. A reprint of the 1982 edition, this book describes the physics of lasers, and contains a description of all major types of lasers—only the description of the X-ray laser is out of date. There is also a long list of laser applications. It is very accessible and informative.

Iannini, Robert E. *Build Your Own Working Fiberoptic, Infrared, and Laser Space-Age Projects.* Blue Ridge Summit, Pa.: Tab Books, 1987. For those truly interested in learning about the physics of lasers, there is no better way to learn than by doing.

Kock, Winston E. *Lasers and Holography: An Introduction to Coherent Optics.* Mineola, N.Y.: Dover Publications, 1981. This introduction to holography, written for the general reader, spends much of the book describing the fundamental properties of light that make holography possible. It is an excellent place to begin a serious study of holography.

Maiman, Theodore H. "Stimulated Optical Radiation in Ruby." *Nature,* 187 (1960): pp. 493–494. This extremely brief and historically important article describes the first successful laser experiment.

Taylor, Nick. *Laser: The Inventor, The Nobel Laureate, and the Thirty-Year Patent War.* New York: Simon & Schuster, 2000. A carefully researched story about politics, science, business, law, love, and a fearless inventor, the author tells the story of the fight over patent rights to the laser in its historical context. Fascinating reading.

Townes, Charles. *How the Laser Happened: Adventures of a Scientist.* New York: Oxford University Press, 1999. Shortly before Nick Taylor released his book and long after patent rights were awarded to Gordon Gould, the inventor of the laser, Charles Townes, Nobel laureate and would-be inventor of the laser, wrote this book to tell his side of the story. It is an interesting book that is best read after Taylor's book.

WORLD WIDE WEB SITES

Although there are a great many Web sites devoted to lasers, many of them are commercial in nature and not particularly informative, others are quite technical, but a few are outstanding. Here are some of the outstanding ones:

Caltech Media Relations. "Laser Points to the Future at Palomar." Available online. URL: http://pr.caltech.edu/media/Press_Releases/PR12613. html. Accessed November 2004. An interesting summary of how adaptive optics has been employed on the huge Hale telescope on Mount Palomar. There is also a link to pictures showing a laser in use with the Hale telescope.

Corning Cable Systems. "Basic Principles of Fiber Optics." Available online. URL: http://www.corningcablesystems.com/web/college/fibertutorial.nsf/ introfro? OpenForm accessed September 17, 2005. An accessible, well-written overview of fiber optic technology. (Corning is a leader in the field.) Each chapter is followed by a multiple choice quiz.

Goldwasser, Samuel M. "Sam's Laser FAQ." Available online. URL: http:// repairfaq.cis.upenn.edu/Misc/lasersam.htm. Accessed September 17, 2005. This mighty Web site may be the best online resource for anyone interested in learning about lasers. The site is designed for hobbyists and experimenters, but it will be of interest to anyone interested in an introduction to the theory of lasers or in learning how to tinker with them. There is also a substantial amount of information about laser safety, although the best, and safest, way to learn to experiment with lasers is still to experiment with someone who already has some experience with these devices.

Nanosight Video Gallery. Available online. URL:http://nanosight.co.uk/ media/videogallery.htm. Accessed September 17, 2005. These are videos from the archives of the company that invented the Halo LM10 (described in chapter 11). They show nanoscale particles illuminated by a laser beam undergoing Brownian motion.

National Academies Press. "AMO Science Improving Health." Available online. URL: http://www.nap.edu/html/atoms_molecules/13-20.pdf. Accessed September 17, 2005. AMO is short for "atoms, molecules, and optical physics," and this article describes some of the ways that lasers and a few other technologies are used in the field of medicine. It is easy reading, and it is full of information.

Outwater, Christopher, and Van Hamersveld. "Practical Holography." Available online. URL: http://www.holo.com/holo/book/book.html#bascom. Accessed September 17, 2005. This site seems to be permanently unfinished. Some of the links do not work, and some of the print is difficult to read. It is, nevertheless, an excellent source of information about holography, as good as or better than any other Web-based source.

Vilnrotter, Simon, and Yan Vilnrotter. "The Power Spectrum of Pulse Position Modulation with Dead Time and Pulse Jitter." Available online. URL: http://tmo.jpl.nasa.gov/progress_report/42-133/133C.pdf. Accessed May 11, 2006.

Walter, Katie. "The X-Ray Laser: From Underground to Tabletop." Available online. URL: http://www.llnl.gov/str/Dunn.html. Accessed September 17, 2005. This is an excellent and completely accessible description of work done on the X-ray laser at Lawrence Livermore Laboratory, one of the great research centers in the United States.

INDEX

Italic page numbers indicate illustrations.